GENESIS

Secrets of Creation

GENESIS

Secrets of Creation

The First Book of Moses

Eleven lectures given in Munich,
16–26 August 1910

RUDOLF STEINER

RUDOLF STEINER PRESS

Rudolf Steiner Press
Hillside House, The Square
Forest Row, East Sussex
RH18 5ES

www.rudolfsteinerpress.com

This edition published by Rudolf Steiner Press 2002

First published in English by Anthroposophical Publishing Co., London 1959, and reprinted by Rudolf Steiner Press in 1982

Originally published in German under the title *Die Geheimnisse der biblischen Schöpfungsgeschichte* (Volume 122 in the *Rudolf Steiner Gesamtausgabe* or Collected Works) by Rudolf Steiner Verlag, Dornach. This authorized translation, based on the 4th revised edition (1961), is published by kind permission of the Rudolf Steiner Nachlassverwaltung, Dornach

Translated by Pauline Wehrle
Translation © Rudolf Steiner Press 2002

A catalogue record for this book is available from the British Library

ISBN 1 85584 102 9

Cover art by Anne Stockton; cover design by Andrew Morgan
Typeset by DP Photosetting, Aylesbury, Bucks.
Printed and bound in Great Britain by Cromwell Press Limited, Trowbridge, Wilts.

Contents

Saturn being *(laila)*. The activity of the hierarchies and their portrayal in the story of creation.

warmth) on the sixth 'day'. Jehovah-Elohim did not
make him into a being of air until after the sixth 'day' of
creation. The sinking down of the human being out of
the earth's periphery through the luciferic influence.
The further condensation to water and solid matter and
the descent of the human being of flesh.

Introduction

Readers opening a book entitled *Genesis—Secrets of Creation* and expecting to find a philosophical or theological investigation will be surprised by something quite different here. In the very first lecture, given more than 90 years ago, Rudolf Steiner shows clearly that he wishes to enter the realm of Creation through the medium of the creative processes in the power of the Word. Demonstrating an amazing knowledge of the Hebrew language he is able to describe how the creative power hidden in the interplay of consonants and vowels in every word can give us a clear picture of those creative forces which shape cosmos and earth.

Like his original audience we, as readers, are drawn into those creative processes. Prepared thus by the first lecture we can behold in the second the growth of the creative tension between the heavens and the earth. Cosmic powers begin to form earth existence, but this does not happen at the mere flick of a divine finger. The third lecture shows that the musical scale of seven aeons is needed in order that the song of earth existence can unfold out of its cosmic origins.

In the fourth lecture we are made aware that behind the phenomena of warmth, air, water and earth, as well as light, sound and life, spiritual beings are at work. We are led to behold those hierarchical beings who are hidden behind the seemingly naïve words of the first chapters of Genesis.

On coming to the fifth lecture we are made aware that not all the hierarchical beings are of a progressive nature. There also exist retarded creator beings whose work is obstructive. Yet these beings, too, fulfil an essential task in the labour of creation. The creative tension first pointed out in the second lecture can now be seen as a fundamental ingredient of any creation.

Out of such tension a new world can be born. Having established this, Rudolf Steiner then points out in the sixth lecture that man could only be created once the seven elohim had become a unity: Jehovah-Elohim. This union enabled them to act not merely out of the sum total of their powers but out of a potentizing of the power of each by that of all his fellow creators. This new creator being was able to create man as a first beginning of a new hierarchy to come.

By the description of the creation of the sensory organs we are made aware in the seventh lecture that due to the gift of his senses man can become a conscious being. The precondition enabling such a gift to be bestowed is that the hierarchical beings in question are those who have attained a higher consciousness. In consequence of this, it is possible for man, too, born out of their creative forces, to become progressively a soul/spiritual being who can attain to ever higher levels of consciousness.

This is shown in the eighth lecture. The counterpart of man's growing mastery of conscious experience is his evolution from a being of warmth through ever denser stages of existence until the present stage of physical humanity in which he has a body of flesh and bone.

In the ninth lecture we are shown that during a time of accelerated hardening of the earth only the sturdiest representatives of the human race could stay whilst all the others had to move, in spiritual form, to the planets until this crisis point in earth evolution had passed. However, as a result of this crisis the earthly human being was able to regain some of his cosmic origin in the manifoldness of races, languages and peoples which began to repopulate the earth when the exiled souls were able to return to this planet. It was a planet which had become so earthly that human bodies would fall into dust once the soul/spirit being had to leave them in death.

Densification of the human body also made it impossible for the human being to remain androgynous as had hitherto been the case. Two genders were now necessary, male and female, but the earthly gender was complemented in that the etheric body in the man was female and in the woman male. It is in the realm of the etheric life forces that outer human existence can be complemented by an inner half. This inner half is the hidden staircase by which human beings will eventually be able to regain their cosmic wholeness and once more find access to that part of the divine creator force which withdrew from its creative work for a period in order to unfold future creative gifts. The union of the human being with the being of Christ is the key which will give humanity access to those future steps of development. Christ is the Lord of the Sabbath not only in its earthly dimension (Math.12,8) but also in its cosmic aspect (as shown in the tenth lecture).

★

The first part of this Introduction has attempted to follow the thought processes through which Rudolf Steiner guides his audience during this series of lectures. The purpose of this was to highlight the fact that these lectures given in 1910 ultimately belong with all those in which Rudolf Steiner pointed to the reappearance of the Christ in the etheric realm. Time and again between 1908 and 1923 he pointed out that the working of the Christ had entered the realm of the forces of life and was thereby opening to man the way to a conscious beholding of the creative forces which weave through all life—just as 1900 years earlier, through his entry into a physical body, Christ had opened the way for a conscious beholding and mastering of earth existence. The frequency of such lectures and indications by Rudolf Steiner peaked in the year 1910.

This faculty which began to develop was totally new, and rather disconcerting at that, for when human beings start to realize that they have begun to possess the gift of seeing the inner life processes of nature and especially of man they might initially experience themselves as peeping through the keyhole into a forbidden chamber. Only in so far as the soul can battle through to an entirely selfless love can it take this step unscathed.

These lectures on Genesis offered Steiner a unique opportunity to lead people in an entirely objective way into the secrets of the creative life forces while making them aware of the conditions ruling this path as well as of its wonders and hurdles. Since this way of teaching is also an entirely discrete one it respects the freedom of the individual in an exemplary way. Attempting to tread the path of consciously beholding etheric reality together with a well-prepared group of people is even today, nearly 100 years later, a true adventure. One has to learn how to step on to holy ground.

*

It is very significant that Rudolf Steiner gave these lectures immediately after the first performance of 'The Portal of Initiation'. In this first of his mystery dramas, as well as in the following three, he attempted to show how human destinies are moulded, purified and transformed when individuals begin to step beyond the threshold of physical earth existence. These lectures on Genesis unfold in the afterglow of that great new step in the life and work of Rudolf Steiner, and he refers to it time and again.

It is good that in this new edition in English the lecture relating to that performance is placed at the end of the book rather than in its historically correct position at the beginning. This may help readers realize out of their work with the secrets of creator life, the secrets of Genesis, that where these life forces are taken hold of consciously on an inner path of striving towards initiation they will bring totally new aspects and developments into the life of the individual and that of his or her life community.

Baruch Luke Urieli

Lecture 1, 17 August 1910[1]

The Mystery of the Primordial Word

If anyone who has a background of spiritual science and has absorbed something of what anthroposophy can tell us about the evolution of our world is able to find the way into those tremendous opening words of our Bible, it should be like entering an entirely new spiritual dimension.[2]

There is probably no account of human evolution so open to misinterpretation as this document usually known as Genesis, the description of the creation of the world in six or seven days. If a person of modern times calls to mind, in one of the languages spoken today, the words 'In the beginning God created the heaven and the earth', what they contain for him can be termed hardly a reflection, barely a shadow of what lived in the ancient Hebrews when they opened their souls to the opening words of the Bible. In fact, with regard to this particular document, the least possible importance attaches to finding the equivalent modern words to put in the place of the ancient ones; and it is far more important that we prepare ourselves through anthroposophy to feel at least something of the mood which lived in the hearts and minds of the ancient Hebrew scholars when they brought to life within themselves the words: *B'reshit bara elohim et hashamayim v'et ha'aretz.*[3]

What was it like—this whole inner world which scholars experienced in the moments when these words flashed through their souls? We can only compare it with what can come alive in the soul of a person when he receives the pictures experienced by a seer who can see into the spiritual world. For what, after all, *is* being described to us through what we call spiritual science? We realize that these descriptions are the outcome of seership, of the living intuitions which the seer receives when, having freed himself from the conditions of sense perception and of the intellect bound up with the physical body, he looks with spiritual organs into the spiritual world. If he wants to translate what he sees there into the languages of the physical world, he can only do so in pictures, and if his descriptive powers suffice, he will do it in pictures which are able to awaken in his hearers a mental image corresponding to what he himself sees in the spiritual worlds. The resulting experience must, however, not be mistaken for a description of things and events of the physical sense world, and we must be aware the whole time that we are having dealings with an entirely different realm—one which does indeed underlie and maintain the ordinary sense world and the mental images, impressions and perceptions which belong there, but which does not actually identify with it at all.

If we want to portray the origin of this our sense world including that of the human being himself, our ideas must not remain confined to the sense world. No science equipped solely with ideas taken from the world of the senses can reach the origins of sense existence. For sense existence is rooted in the supersensible element, and although we can go a long way back historically and even geologically, we must realize that if we want to arrive at the origins, we must, at a certain point in the primordial past, leave the sphere of the sense world and rise up into regions that can only be grasped supersensibly. What we call Genesis does not begin with the portrayal of anything to do with sense perceptions, a portrayal of anything that could be seen with eyes in the external physical world. In the course of these lectures we shall have ample chance to become convinced that we should be quite mistaken to take the words of the first sections of Genesis as referring to things or events which can be seen with the physical eye. Therefore as long as you connect the words 'heaven and earth' with anything containing a residue of the sensuously visible, you have not reached the dimension to which the first sections of Genesis are referring. Today there is practically no other way of throwing light upon the world it describes except through spiritual science. But with the spiritual scientific method a certain possibility is there to approach what we might call the mystery of these primordial words with which the Bible opens, and get a feeling for their content.

What is their special character? If I may put it abstractly to begin with, their secret lies in the fact that they are written in the Hebrew tongue, a language which works upon the soul quite differently than any modern language can. Although the Hebrew of these early chapters may not work in the same way today, it did at one time have the effect that when a letter was sounded it called up a picture in the soul. Pictures arose in the soul of someone who entered with living interest into the words and let them work upon him—pictures harmoniously arranged, organic pictures, pictures which may be compared with what the seer can still see today when he proceeds from the realm of the senses to the realm of the supersensible. The Hebrew language or, to be more exact, the language of the first chapters of the Bible, enabled the soul to call up pictorial images very similar to those the seer encounters when, freed from his body, he is able to look into supersensible regions of existence.

Therefore if we want to reach in some measure a living picture of these powerful primordial words it is essential to forgo all the pale and shadowy impressions which any modern language can have on us and get an idea of the tremendously alive, creatively stimulating power inherent in any of the sound sequences in this ancient tongue. So it is of immense importance that in the course of these lectures we really do attempt to conjure up those very pictures which arose in the Hebrew scholars of old when a particular sound worked creatively within them and the corresponding image arose. You see from this that there has to be an entirely different way of penetrating into this document than all those paths chosen today to understand ancient writings.

This gives you an indication of our line of approach. It will be a slow and gradual process to acquire a living picture of what lived in the ancient Hebrew sages when they let those most powerful words work on them which, as words, do at least still exist in the world. Our next task will be to stick as little as possible to what we already know, and free ourselves as much as we can from the ideas we previously held when we talked about heaven and earth, the gods, creation and a primordial beginning. The more we can liberate ourselves from the feelings we had towards these words the better we shall be able to penetrate into the spirit of a document which arose out of quite different soul conditions than those of today. Above all we must come to an agreement as to what we are talking about in the spiritual scientific sense when we speak about the opening words of the Bible.

You know of course that it is possible for today's clairvoyant researcher to describe from a certain aspect the origin and evolution of our earth and of human existence. In my book *An Outline of Esoteric Science*[4] I endeavoured to describe how the earth, as the scene, the planetary scene of the human race, gradually came into being through the three preliminary stages of evolution, the Saturn, Sun and Moon stages. You will certainly be able to recapture, at least in broad outline, what was described there. The question is at what point in the spiritual scientific account should we place the soul impression made on us by the mighty word *b'reshit*? Where does it belong?

Let us be clear about the way in which we can visualize the

Saturn, Sun and Moon existences. If we look back for a moment to ancient Saturn we picture it as a cosmic body which does not yet possess anything of what we are used to calling material attributes. Of all that we find in our own environment it has only the element of warmth; warmth or fire, the mobile element of warmth. No air or water or solid earth is as yet to be found upon ancient Saturn; so that even where it is densest it is living, weaving warmth. Then, as we know, existence advances to the so-called Sun stage. To that mobile warmth a kind of air or gaseous element is added; and we have a true picture of the planetary condition of the Sun if we regard the elements of which it is composed as consisting of an interweaving and combining of gaseous, airy elements and warmth elements. The third condition in the evolution of our earth is the so-called Moon stage. Here, what we can call the element of water is added to the warmth and air. During the old Moon stage there is as yet nothing of what in our present earth stage we call solid. However, during the Moon stage a special event occurs: the homogeneous character of the life of the planet now divides into two. Looking back upon old Saturn we see it as a unified state of weaving warmth, and old Sun appears as an interweaving of the elements of gas and warmth. During the Moon existence a split occurs between what is of the nature of the Sun and what is of the nature of the Moon. It is only when we come to the fourth stage of our planetary evolution that we see the solid earth element added to the earlier elemental conditions of warmth, air and water. So that this solid element could occur in the life of our planet the division which had previously taken place during the Moon stage had to be repeated. Once again the sun element had to withdraw from the earth nature of the planet. Thus at a certain moment in the evolution of our planet the denser earthly element and the more delicate airy sun element separate out from a unified planetary condition where there was an interweaving of the elements of fire, air and water. It is only in this newly-arisen earthly element that a densification into the solid element could occur.

Let us picture this moment when the sun withdraws from its unified planetary existence and from now on sends its forces down to the earthly element from outside. Let us bear in mind that this is what made it possible that within the earthly element the solid element—which in a material sense we call solid—could begin to condense. If we focus on this moment we have the point of time at which Genesis, the Bible, begins. This is what it is describing. We must not associate with the opening words of Genesis the abstract, shadowy ideas we think of when we utter the words 'In the beginning'. Compared with what the ancient Hebrew sage felt it would be unspeakably poverty-stricken. If we want to fill our souls in the proper way with the sound *b'reshit*—in the beginning—we must conjure up the whole picture of that twofoldness which came into being through the separating of sun nature from earth nature, everything that was there at the actual moment when the separation had just taken place. And further, we must also be aware that throughout the whole of the Saturn, Sun and Moon stages evolution was guided and carried by spiritual beings; and that what we call the elements of warmth, air and water are always only the outer expression, the outer garments of the spiritual beings who are the reality of evolution. Even when we behold the condition existing at the moment of separation between the elements of sun and earth, and picture it to ourselves in thoughts full of material images, we must not forget that in all our picturing of the elements of water, air and fire we are seeing the expressions of the flowing world of spirituality which, having progressed through the Saturn, Sun and Moon stages, has now reached this particular point in evolution.

Let us place before us the picture of an immense cosmic

globe composed of weaving elements of water, air and gas, and fire, a globe which splits into a sun part and an earth part; but let us keep hold of the picture that everything we imagine as material elements is only a means of expression for spiritual beings. Let us imagine that from this substantial habitation woven of the elements of water, air and warmth the countenances of spiritual beings weaving within it look out upon us, manifesting themselves to us in an element we grasp in thoughts of material images. Let us imagine we have before us spiritual beings looking towards us and who, with the force of their soul/spiritual nature are organizing cosmic bodies through the medium of warmth, air and water. Let us stop and look at this picture!

We have a picture of a sheath of elements which, if we want to have an approximate visual picture of it we can visualize as a snail shell, but a shell not formed of solid matter like a snail's but woven out of the most delicate elements of water, air and fire. Let us think of spiritual beings looking at us in the form of countenances who both use this sheath as a means of revelation and are themselves a force of revelation, a force which, from the hidden world of the supersensible, pokes forth into manifestation, if I may use such an expression.

If you call up in your mind's eye this picture which I have just endeavoured to paint for you, this living movement of spirit in a material element, and also envisage the inner soul force which causes it to happen then, concentrating on this to the exclusion of everything else, you will have something approximating what lived in an ancient Hebrew sage when the sounds *b'reshit* entered his soul. *Bet*, the first letter, called up the weaving together of the substance of the outer shell, *resh*, the second accompanying sound, called up the countenances of the spiritual beings who did the weaving within the shell, and *shin*, the third sound, called up the prickly force that was working its way out to manifestation.[5]

This is approximately how we arrive at the principle behind such a description. When we reach this we are able to appreciate something of the spirit of this language which combined with a creativity of soul of which the people of today, with their abstract languages, can have no idea.

Let us now imagine ourselves concentrating fully on the moment in time prior to the physical coagulation, the physical densification of our earth, for this is what I want to describe. If we imagine this as vividly as we can, we shall have to admit that if we want to describe what is taking place there we cannot apply any of the thought images we use today to describe processes in the external sense world. Therefore it is utterly pretentious to associate with the second word we meet in Genesis any external factor however closely it may resemble what we understand today as 'creating'. In that way we shall not get near to the meaning of this word. Where can we turn for help? The word does in fact imply something which lies very near the boundary where things of a sensuous nature pass over directly into the realm of the spiritual/supersensible. And anyone who wants to grasp the meaning of the word which is usually translated as 'created' (In the beginning God created...) must not associate it in any way with a creative activity which can be seen with ordinary physical sense perception.

My dear friends, look at your own being. Imagine you have been asleep for a while, and on waking you do not open your eyes to things around you but, through an inner activity, fill your mind with certain mental images. Visualize this inner activity, this fertile thinking which, as if by magic, conjures up soul substance from the depths of your soul. If you like you can use the word 'excogitate' for this conjuring up of soul substance out of the depths into the field of consciousness; and now think of this activity, which human beings can do only in their mental images, as an activity that is actually on a cosmically creative scale. Instead of your own inner experience of thinking imagine cosmic thinking, then you have the content of the second word of Genesis, *bara*. Think of it as spiritually as you can, and bring it as close as you can to the life of thought which you see in your mind's eye, as close as you can!

And now imagine that during your cogitating you bring two sets of mental images to mind. To make such a remote idea as clear as possible, think of a person who has been asleep and when he wakes up two things occur to him and he thinks about these two different kinds of things. Suppose the one kind of thought is the picture either of some activity or of some external thing or being which does not enter his consciousness by way of outer perception but through thinking, through creative soul activity. Suppose the second set of ideas occuring to the individual is a desire, something which the person's whole disposition and constitution can prompt him to will. So we have elements both of thought and of desire arising in our inner soul activity. Now imagine this inner activity happening not in the human soul but in the beings called in Genesis the elohim. Instead of the single human soul imagine a multiplicity of spiritual beings thinking, and in a similar way calling up out of their inner being two sets of images which I would like to compare with what I have just been describing to you—an element of pure thought and an element of desire. So, instead of imagining a human soul thinking, we think of an organization of cosmic beings calling up in a similar way—except that their thinking is cosmic—two sets of mental images, one of the nature of thought, that is, one which reveals something by manifesting itself outwardly, and another of the nature of desire, full of inner activity. So let us picture the cosmic beings called the elohim thinking in this fashion, and realize that this is the picture of 'created', *bara*. And then let us imagine by means of this creative thinking two such sets of mental images arising, one which is more of the nature of outer revelation, external manifestation, and another which is inwardly alive and active; then we have approximately the two sets of mental images which arose in the souls of the ancient Hebrew sages when the words *hashamayim* and *ha'retz*—represented nowadays by 'heaven and earth' sounded within them. Let us try as hard as we can to forget what present-day people think of as 'heaven and earth', and try to bring the two sets of mental images to mind: the set which tends more to manifest and to call forth an outer effect, and the set which is inwardly active, tending to remain as an inner experience. Then we have the essence of *hashamayim* and *ha'aretz*.

And the elohim themselves, what kind of beings are they? In the course of these lectures we shall get to know them better and describe them in terms of spiritual science; but for the present let us try to reach in some measure the meaning of this primordial word 'elohim'. If you want a picture of what lived in the souls of the ancient Hebrew sages when they used this word you must realize that in those days people were thoroughly aware that our earth evolution had its own meaning, its specific goal. What is this purpose, this goal?

Our earth evolution can have a meaning only if during its course something arises which was not there before. A perpetual repetition of what was already there would be a meaningless existence, and the ancient Hebrew sages would have regarded earth genesis as without meaning unless they had known that the earth, after it had progressed through previous stages, had to bring something new into existence which had never been there before. Earth evolution provided the possibility for something new, namely that human beings became exactly the kind of beings they have become in the course of this evolution. In none of the earlier stages of evolution was man present as the being he is today, the being he will increasingly become in far-reaching future perspectives, for that was not possible in earlier stages. Those spiritual beings who guided and supported the manifestations of evolution we call the Saturn, Sun and Moon stages were of a different nature from man—for the moment we will not enter into the question of whether they were higher or lower. What is the best way to come to an understanding of the nature of those beings who were at work in the fiery, gaseous and watery elements of the earlier stages of existence composing the Saturn, Sun and Moon existence and the beginning of earth existence? How can we draw near to them?

We should have to go into a very great number of things to get anywhere near an understanding of these beings. To begin with, however, we can acquaint ourselves with one aspect of them, and that will suffice to bring us at least one step nearer to the potent conception of the primordial Bible words. Let us consider those beings who in a certain sense were nearest to man at the moment he was brought forth from what had evolved during the ancient Saturn, Sun and Moon stages. Let us ask these beings about their actual intentions. Let us ask them what their will and purpose was. Then we shall be able to get at least some idea of their nature. What was it they intended doing? They could do many things; in the course of their evolution they had acquired capacities in one direction or another. One of them could do this, another that. But we understand the nature of these beings best if we realize that at the time we are now considering they were working as a group towards a common goal. It is, at a higher level, as though a group of human beings, each with their own special skill, were to co-operate today. Each of them has an ability in some direction, and they now say to one another: You can do this, I can do that, and he can do the other. Let us pool all our activities to carry out a joint action in which each of us can be active. So let us imagine such a group of human beings, each of whom has a different capacity, but who have a common aim. What they intend bringing into being is not yet there. The object of their endeavours consists at the moment only of an aim, and does not exist as yet. What is there is a multiplicity, and the unit lives initially in the form of an ideal. Now think of a group of spiritual beings who have passed through the evolution of Saturn, Sun and Moon, each one of whom has a specific ability and who, at the moment I have indicated, come to the decision: We will combine our activities for a common end, we will all work in the one direction. And the picture of this goal arose before each of them. What was this goal? It was man, earthly man!

Thus earthly man existed as the goal among a group of divine/spiritual beings who had resolved to combine their several skills to arrive at something which they themselves did not have at all, but which they were able to create by combined effort. If you put together all that I have described to you—the elemental sheath and spiritual beings active within it thinking cosmic thoughts in the form of two complexes, one inwardly active and the other manifesting outwardly—and then ascribe the common purpose I have just mentioned to those spiritual beings whose countenances look out as it were from out of the elemental sheath, then you have what lived in the hearts of the Hebrew sages of old with the word *elohim*. Thus we have brought before us in picture form what lives in all these all-powerful primordial words.

So let us forget all that a modern person can feel and think when he pronounces the words 'In the beginning God created the heaven and the earth'. Bearing in mind all that I have told you today, try to put this picture before you: There is a sphere in which fiery, gaseous and watery elements weave, and within this active weaving, elemental sphere there is a group of spiritual beings who are engaged in thinking creatively, and the goal of their creative thinking is to direct the whole force of their joint activity towards the image of man. The first fruit of their thinking is the conception of something manifesting itself outwardly and of something else inwardly active: In the elemental sheath the primordial spirits brought into being out of themselves the creative thought of a process outwardly manifesting, a process inwardly active.

Try to picture in these terms what is said in the opening lines of the Bible; for here we have the foundation of all we shall be looking at in the next few days regarding the true significance of those all-powerful primordial words which are for humankind such a tremendous revelation, the revelation of our own origin.

Ha'aretz and Hashamayim

In a good many places in the course of these lectures—as well as elsewhere in our anthroposophical discussions—it may well appear, particularly to the outside world, who are hardly aware of the kind of feelings that prevail in our circles, as if I rather enjoyed it when I am pressed to set myself up in apparent opposition to modern science. This is a point on which I am particularly anxious to avoid misunderstanding. I assure you that it costs me a real effort to do anything of the sort, and that I only do it at those precise points where I myself am able to carry further what science has to say. My sense of responsibility is such that it will not permit me to bring forward anything that conflicts with the opinions of modern science unless I am able to cite what science itself has to say on the subject. No one having such an attitude could possibly approach the all-important matters which are to occupy us in the next few days without the deepest sense of awe and the responsibility that goes with it.

Unfortunately it has to be said that as regards the questions we shall have to face, modern science is bound to break down altogether. Modern scientists are not even in a position to know why this should be so, and why their science must necessarily prove so hopelessly amateurish regarding the great and real problems of life and of existence. So although in a short course of lectures it is obviously not possible to engage in polemics about every detail, please take it for granted that with regard to all I say I am fully aware of the modern scientific outlook on these subjects. I must confine myself as far as possible to what is positive, and trust that in a circle of anthroposophists this will always be understood.

Yesterday I endeavoured to show you that those tremendous primordial words with which the Bible opens— words which are in a language of quite a different nature from modern tongues—can only be rightly interpreted if we try to forget the attitude of feeling we have acquired in response to the usual modern renderings. For the language in which these all-powerful words of creation were originally given to us does indeed possess the characteristic that the very nature of its sounds directs our hearts and minds towards those pictures which arise before the eye of the seer when he contemplates the moment of the welling forth of the sense perceptible part of our world out of the supersensible element. There is such power, such force in every single sound in which the primordial origin of our earth existence is set before us. In the course of these lectures we shall often have cause to refer to the character of this language; today, however, let us confine ourselves to some of the first essentials.

You know that in the Bible, after the words I endeavoured to sketch for you yesterday, there comes a description of one of the complexes arising out of the creative thinking of the gods. I told you that we have to picture that, as if out of cosmic memory, two complexes arose. One was a complex which may be compared to the nature of thoughts which can arise in us, the other to our desire or will nature. The one complex contains all that drives towards outer manifestation, tends as it were to proclaim its force—*hashamayim*. The other complex—*ha'aretz*—consists of an inner activity filled with desire. Then we are told of certain qualities of this inwardly active, enlivening element, and these are indicated in the Bible with sounds which portray their character. We are told that this inwardly active element was in a condition described as *tohu wa'bohu*—'without form and void'.[1] To understand what is meant by *tohu wa'bohu* we must paint a picture of it; and we shall only succeed in this if out of our spiritual scientific knowledge we call to mind what it was that, after its passage through the Saturn, Sun and Moon stages, re-emerged and surged through space as our earth existence, as our planet earth.

I pointed out yesterday that what we call the solid condition, namely that which offers resistance to our senses, did not exist during the Saturn, Sun and Moon stages; all that existed then were the elements of fire or warmth, gas or air, and water. Basically it was not until the planet earth stage emerged that the solid element was added to the previous elemental conditions. So that when the moment occurred that we described yesterday, of the sun beginning to split off from the earth, this was the moment when the elements of warmth, air and water began mutually to interpenetrate. What we have to imagine as this preliminary surging interpenetration is the meaning of the phrase 'without form and void', though this is a quite inexact expression, and it is eloquently rendered by the succession of sounds *tohu wa'bohu*. What then does *tohu wa'bohu* mean? If we picture what can be stirred to life in us by these sounds, it is something like the following.

The sound which resembles our own T calls up a picture of forces diverging from a central point in every direction of space. Thus in the moment one utters the T sound one has the picture of forces raying out from a central point in every direction into infinite distances. So we have to imagine the elements of warmth, air and water permeating and inter-penetrating each other, and within them a raying out as from a centre in all directions, and this raying out would be there if we only heard the first part of the sound structure, *tohu*. What does the second part of the phrase signify? It expresses the very opposite of what I have just described. *Bet*, the sound which resembles our B, has the character of calling forth in our imagination the picture of an enormous sphere, a hollow sphere, with yourself inside it, and rays proceeding from every point inside this sphere towards the centre. Thus you imagine a point in space with forces streaming out in all directions, and this is *tohu*; then these forces are arrested as it were by an outer spherical enclosure and turned back on themselves from every direction of space, and this is *bohu*. Then, if you imagine this, and think of all the rays of force, filled with the three elemental entities of warmth, air and water, then you know the nature of the complex of inner, animated activity. The very sound structure itself shows us how the being of the elements was administered and ruled by the elohim.

How far has this brought us? We shall not understand the whole enormous dramatic process of the seven days of creation unless we bring these details to mind. If we do so, then the whole thing will present itself to us as a powerful cosmic drama. What are we being told? Let us remember once again that in all that is conveyed by the verb *bara*—in the beginning the gods 'created'—we are concerned with a soul/spiritual activity. I compared this yesterday to the thought complexes which are called up in our own souls. So we may think of the elohim reposing in space, and of what is indicated by 'created', *bara*, as a cosmic kind of thinking. What the elohim call up in thought is expressed by *hashamayim* and *ha'aretz*—an outward raying and an inner activating. Now, however, our attention is drawn to something else of great significance. To have as close a comparison as possible picture yourselves in the moment of awakening. Groups of ideas arise in your mind. In the elohim's minds *hashamayim* and *ha'aretz* arise.

However, we emphasized yesterday that these elohim came over to earth evolution at the stage to which they had evolved during the Saturn, Sun and Moon evolutions. So they were in a similar situation to you when you wake up and bring groups of thoughts to mind. You can contemplate these thoughts in a kind of soul/spiritual way, you can tell what they are like. You can say: 'When I wake up in the morning and recall what was previously in my mind and what I am now calling up, I can describe it.' It was approximately the same for the elohim when they said to themselves: 'Let us now think creatively about what arises in our souls when we recall all that took place during the old Saturn, Sun and Moon evolutions. Let us see what it looks like when we remember it.' What it looked like is described in the words *tohu wa'bohu,* and could be expressed by the picture I gave you of rays streaming out from a centre into space and back again in such a way that the elements interacted in these rays of force. Thus the elohim could say, roughly: 'This is what things look like after we have brought them to this point. This is how they re-emerge.'

So as to understand what comes next, and what is usually rendered in modern languages in the words 'darkness was upon the face of the waters' we must consider something else. We must once more turn our attention to the course of evolutionary events before the earth stage began.

First we have the Saturn stage working its way into the element of fire. Then the Sun stage is added, with its element of air. In my *Outline of Esoteric Science* you can read up, however, that something else was connected with the arrival of air. The element of gas or air was not the only thing that was added to the element of warmth. That is, so to speak, the coarsening of the warmth element. The finer warmth element of ancient Saturn was coarsened to the element of gas. But each such coarsening is connected with the arising of something of a finer nature. Just as a coarsening to the element of gas is the equivalent of a descending process, there is also an ascent to the element of light. So when we proceed from old Saturn to old Sun we have to say that Saturn consists solely of the element of weaving warmth, whereas during the Sun stage something coarser, the gaseous element, is added, but also the element of light, which enables the warmth and the gas to reveal themselves in outward radiance.

If we now look at the one group of thoughts, the one expressed by *ha'aretz*, usually translated as 'earth', we have to ask how the elohim, when they had brought it alive in their memory, would have described it. They could not have described it as a revival of what already existed in old Sun. For the element of light was not there. That had withdrawn. *Ha'aretz* had therefore become one-sided. It did not bring with it the light but only the coarser elements, water, air and warmth. True, the light was not absent in what is expressed by *hashamayim*, but *hashamayim* is the sun nature which issues from the other complex of thoughts. In this other complex there was no refinement of the elements, there was no light. So we may say that in one of the complexes the warmth, air and water elements were all mixed together in the way indicated by *tohu wa'bohu*. These elements were laid bare and lacked the light which had entered evolution with the old Sun. They remained dark and had none of the sun nature about them, for that had withdrawn from them with *hashamayim*. Thus the progression to the earth stage means nothing else than that the light, which the planet still had so long as the sun remained united with it, had now withdrawn, and a dark mass of warmth, air and water elements had been left behind as *ha'aretz*.

So now we have a more detailed picture of the thoughts of the elohim. But we shall never be able to picture them in the right way unless we are conscious all the time that the elements of air, water and warmth are in fact also the external expression of spiritual beings. It would not be quite correct to say their 'garment', for we should think of it more as an outer manifestation. Therefore all that we call air, water and warmth are basically *maya*, illusion; they exist only for outer perception, including the perception of the mind's eye. In fact the real nature of these elements is soul/spiritual, and they are an outer manifestation of the soul/spiritual nature of the elohim. However, if we want to know what the elohim look like we must not think of them as looking as yet at all human, for their actual goal was to give man his form and call him into existence in his own individual organization which was about to be created by them in their thoughts. So we must not think of them as human. But we must certainly envisage that there is already in their make-up a kind of split. When we speak of the human being today we do not understand him at all unless we distinguish between body, soul and spirit. You know what great efforts we anthroposophists make to get a closer understanding of the activity and nature of this trinity in man, his body, soul and spirit. To recognize this unity in trinity first becomes necessary in the case of man, and we should be making the greatest mistake to think of beings before man, the beings whom the Bible calls the elohim, as if they resembled man. Nevertheless in their case we must certainly distinguish between a kind of body and a kind of spirit.

When you distinguish between body and spirit in man you are well aware that even his outer form bears testimony to the fact that his being lives in it in a variety of ways. For instance we do not try to locate man's mind in his hands or legs, but we say that his bodily functions are in his trunk and his limbs, that the organ of his mind is the head, the brain: the brain is the instrument of the mind. This is how we think of the division in the external human form, understanding that some parts are more the expression of the physical body while other parts are more the expression of the spirit.

We have to look upon the elohim in a similar even if not quite the same way. All the surging mass I was talking about can only be correctly understood if it is looked upon as the bodily vehicle of the elohim's soul/spirit nature. Everything presented in the way of the elements of air, warmth and water are the external embodiment of the elohim. But we have to make a further distinction; we have to look upon the watery and gaseous elements as more connected with the bodily and coarser functions of the elohim, and see the warmth element that intermingles with the air and water, this *tohu wa'bohu,* as the element in which what we can call the spirit of the elohim is at work. Just as where man is concerned we say that the more bodily part functions in his trunk and the limbs and the more spiritual part in his head, so, if we look upon the entire cosmos as an embodiment of the elohim, we can say that their more specifically bodily part lived in the air and the water and their spiritual part moved in the warmth. Thus we now see the cosmos itself as an embodiment of the elohim. Having characterized their outer embodiment as a *tohu wa'bohu* of elemental beings, we have localized the active spirit of the elohim in the warmth element intermingling with the elemental beings.

The Bible uses a remarkable phrase to express the relationship of this spiritual part of the elohim to the elements: *Ruach elohim mrachefet*—a remarkable phrase we must go into more closely if we want to understand how the spirit of the elohim intermingled with the other elements.[2] We can only understand the word *rachef* if we enlist the help of everything this word conjured up in the souls of those who heard it.[3] If we simply say 'And the spirit of God moved upon the face of the waters' we have not said anything. We can only arrive at a real elucidation of this verb *rachef* if we imagine a hen sitting on her eggs and the warmth of the hen radiating out over the eggs beneath her. (I know this is a crude illustration, but it does help to bring out the meaning). If you think of the activity of the brooding warmth streaming from the hen into the eggs to bring them to maturity, then you have an idea of the verb used to describe what the spirit does in the element of warmth. It would of course be quite inaccurate to say that the spirit of the elohim 'broods', because what we understand today by the physical activity of brooding is not what is meant. It is far rather the activity of the radiating warmth that is being described. Just as warmth radiates from the hen, the spirit of the elohim radiated by means of the warmth element into the other elements of air and water. When you think of this picture you have an image of what is meant by the words: 'And the spirit of God moved upon the face of the waters.'

Up to a point we have now reconstructed the picture which hovered in the mind of the ancient Hebrew sage when he thought about this primordial state. We have constructed a complex of warmth, air and water intermingling in a spherical form such as I have described *tohu wa'bohu* to be, from which all the light had withdrawn with the *hashamayim*, and this intermingling of the three elemental conditions was inwardly interwoven with darkness. In one of these elements, the warmth, there works the spirituality of the elohim, expanding in all directions with the expanding warmth, and bringing to maturity what is still immature in the dark element.

So when we come to the end of the sentence usually rendered by the words: 'And the spirit of God moved upon the face of the waters' we have a description of one of the parts conveyed in the opening verse of the Bible by *ha'aretz*, namely 'earth'. We have a characterization of what is left behind after *hashamayim* has withdrawn.

Let us now recall the earlier conditions. We can go back from the earth to the stages of the Moon, the Sun and Saturn. Let us go back to the Sun. We know that at that time it was out of the question that there could be a separation between what we today call earth from the sun, therefore it was impossible that the earth could be illuminated by light from outside. That is of course an essential aspect of our life on earth that the light comes to us from outside. If you imagine the earth sphere as enclosed within the Sun, forming part of the Sun and not receiving light but itself forming part of the undivided entity that rayed light out into space, you have a picture of the Sun stage. We can sum it up by saying that then the earth element did not receive light but dispersed it, for it was itself a source of light.

Look at the difference! At the old Sun stage the earth itself participated in shedding light, whereas in its new condition at the earth stage it no longer does so. The earth has surrendered all of the light-giving element and is dependent on receiving light from outside. Light now has to shine into it. That is the essential difference between the earth as it has become in the course of evolution and the Sun stage. With the separation of the sun, of *hashamayim*, the light accompanied it. It is now outside the earth. And the elemental existence which intermingles in *ha'aretz* as *tohu wa'bohu* has no light of its own but only what we can call 'hovered over and warmed through by the spirit of the elohim'. This, however, did not make it bright in itself, but left it dark.

Let us take another look at this elementary existence as a whole. You know of course from earlier lectures that when we enumerate what we call the elemental conditions on earth we begin with the solid element and follow that with water, gas or air, and then warmth. These constitute as it were the densest conditions of matter. But these are not all of them. If we ascend further we meet with finer conditions, but just calling them finer substances does not tell us much about them. The main thing is to recognize them as relatively finer than the denser ones of gas, warmth, and so on. They are usually called etheric conditions, and we have always described light as the first of these. So if we descend from warmth into the next stage below it in density we come to gas, and if we ascend we come to light. Going up a stage beyond light we come to an even finer etheric condition, to something which is not actually directly there in the ordinary sense world. We are only presented with a kind of external reflection of it. From the occult point of view one can say that the forces in this finer ether are those which govern the chemical affinities and combinations of material substances, the organization of matter such as we can observe if, for instance, we place a fine powder on a metal plate and then draw a violin bow down the edge of the plate and obtain the so-called Chladni's plate patterns. What the physical sound produces in the powder is happening of course in space. However, space is differentiated, and is filled with the movement of forces which are more rarefied than light, and which represent at the spiritual level what sound is in the sense world. So when we ascend from warmth to light and from there to this finer element, we can speak of a chemical or sound ether, which contains the forces to differentiate matter, to separate and combine substances, but in reality is of the nature of sound of which the sense perceptible sound heard by the ear is only the outward expression, namely the expression of its passage through the air. This brings us close to this finer element which is above light. So that when we say that the power to manifest outwardly withdrew from the *ha'aretz* with the *hashamayim* we must not think only of what manifests as light but also of the finer etheric element of sound which permeates light.

Just as we go downwards from warmth to air and from there to water we can go upwards from warmth to light and from light to sound, to the element governing chemical substances. And from water we can descend further to the earth element. Where do we arrive if we ascend from the sound ether to an even higher, more rarified etheric condition, which also withdrew with *hashamayim*? We come to the finest etheric state of all, weaving within the sound or chemical ether. If you harken with your spiritual ear in this direction you do not hear a sound vibrating in the air, of course, but you hear the sound which disseminates space, permeates it and organizes substances just as the tone produced by the violin bow organizes the Chladni sound figures. But into this condition brought about by the sound ether there streams an even higher etheric state. This even finer ether permeates the sound ether just as the sound our mouth utters is permeated with the meaning of our thought, turning the sound into word. Try to comprehend what it is that makes a sound into a meaningful word, and then you will have a picture of this finer etheric element moving cosmically through the organizing universal sound, giving it meaning, as it reverberates in space as the creative Word. This Word, streaming through space, pouring itself into the sound ether, is the source of life, is vigorous, vibrant life! Thus what withdrew out of *ha'aretz* with *hashamayim*, what went with the sun as distinct from the lower part, the earth, i.e. the *tohu wa'bohu*, is something which can manifest outwardly as light. But behind the light is spiritual sound, and behind even that is cosmic speech; therefore we may say that the brooding warmth is the first form of expression of the lower spiritual part of the elohim, somewhat as our own life of desire spends itself in the lower part of our soul. The higher spirituality of the elohim which went out with the *hashamayim* lives in the light in spiritual sound, in the spiritual Word, the cosmic Word. These higher qualities can only stream back into the *tohu wa'bohu* again from outside.

Let us now try to get a picture of the whole of what hovered before the soul of the ancient Hebrew sage as the *ha'aretz* and the *hashamayim*. When the forces of spiritual light, of sound, of the forming of the sounds of speech and the creating of words shines on to the earth again, how does it come across? It has the effect of articulate light coming from the sun, as light giving utterance to cosmic speech. So let us think of all the darkness we are presented with in *tohu wa'bohu*, with its intermingling warmth, air and water, let us think of it in its light-forsaken darkness. And then let us think that out of the activity of the elohim, through the creative Word—which, as the highest ether entity, lies behind their activity—there rays in with the light all that streams forth from the Word. How is one to describe what is taking place? The most appropriate way to describe it is to say that the beings who, with *hashamayim* have withdrawn their highest qualities up into the etheric realm, radiated answering light from out of cosmic space into the *tohu wa'bohu*. These are the real facts behind the monumental words: And God said, Let there be light: and there was light in the darkness that was *tohu wa'bohu*. Here you have the picture which hovered before the soul of the ancient Hebrew sage.

So we must think of the beings of the elohim as spread out over the whole cosmos, thinking of this whole cosmos as their body; and the elemental existence in the *tohu wa'bohu* as the lowest form of this body, of the warmth as a somewhat higher form, and the *hashamayim*, which withdrew and now works creatively into the whole formation of the *tohu wa'bohu*, as the form taken by their highest spiritual part.

You now see what I am leading up to—that it was the light-bringing cosmic Word which brought order into the *tohu wa'bohu*, the surging elements, and made it what it later became. Where was the point from which the organizing of the human form took place? There can be no human form such as we have, standing upright on our two legs, making use of our hands the way we do, unless it is organized by forces emanating from the brain. Our human form is organized by the highest spiritual forces streaming forth from our own spirit. What is lower is always organized by what is higher. Thus in the *ha'aretz*, as the body of the elohim as it were, the lower part was organized by the higher bodily part, the *hashamayim*, and the spiritual essence of the elohim working within it. So the highest spirituality of the elohim takes possession of what has been left to itself and organizes it, as expressed by the words: 'The light manifesting in the cosmic Word streams into the darkness.' This is how the *tohu wa'bohu* was organized, raised up from out of the disorder of the elements. So if you think of the *hashamayim* as a kind of head of the elohim and the elements left behind as the trunk and limbs, and these elements, the trunk and limbs, being organized through the power of the head, then you have the actual process. Then you have the human being enlarged as it were to fill the whole cosmos; and in this cosmos he organizes himself out of the spiritual organs contained in *hashamayim*. When we think of all the streams of energy which pour down from the *hashamayim* to the *ha'aretz* we may venture to picture a macrocosmic human being working on his own organization.

So as to paint the picture even more exactly, let us now turn our attention to the human being as he is today. Let us ask ourselves how the human being has become as he is—I mean as he is to the spiritual scientist, not to ordinary science. What is it that has given him the special configuration which distinguishes him from all the other living creatures around him? What is it that actually makes him human, what force is working throughout this human form? Unless you deliberately close your eyes to it, it is very easy to pinpoint what makes him man; it is something he possesses and none of the other creatures around him in earthly existence possess: speech, the sounds of speech. This is what makes us human. Think of the animal form and ask yourselves how it could be raised to the level of the human form. What would have to enter in for it to become human? Let us put the question this way. Let us think of an animal form, and imagine we had to pour something into it, breathe something into it—what would this breath have to contain to make this form begin to speak? It would have to feel changed to the point where it brought forth the sounds of speech. It is the sounds of speech which make the animal form into a human form!

So how can we imagine the picture of the cosmos, create an inner feeling of what it is like? How can we build up a feeling of all the pictures I have presented to you, of all the intricate pictures I have described to you of the life of the elements; how can we create a feeling of all this, create an inner feeling for the structure of the macrocosmic human being? By beginning to feel how the sounds of speech come to life within it. When the sound Ah sounds forth through the air, learn to feel not only its tone but the form it makes, just as the tone of the violin bow drawn down the edge of a metal plate makes a form in the dust. Learn to feel the Ah and the B in their movement through space! Experience them not merely as sound but as form-making; then you will feel what the Hebrew sage felt when the sounds of speech stimulated him to see the pictures I have put before your mind's eye. This was the effect the sounds of speech had. This was why I had to tell you that *Bet* (B) aroused the idea of an enclosing gesture, like a shell shutting something off and enclosing it within. *Resh* (R) stimulated a feeling such as one has when one feels one's head, and *Shin* (S) suggested what I called pricking or poking. This is a thoroughly objective language, a language which, if the soul is receptive, crystallizes into pictures as the sounds are uttered. In the sounds themselves lies the lofty schooling which led the sages to the pictures which crowd in upon the soul of the seer when he enters the supersensible world. The sounds of speech are transmuted into spiritual form and conjure up pictures which come together as a connected whole in the way I have described. What is so significant about this ancient record is that it has been preserved in a language the sounds of which are form-creating, which crystallize in the soul into forms. And these forms are the very pictures which one gets when one penetrates into the supersensible realm out of which the material part of our physical earth planet has evolved. When you realize this you will be filled with a feeling of deep awe and reverence for the way the world has evolved. It will dawn on you that it is truly by no mere chance that this tremendous document of human existence has been transmitted in this script—a script which by means of its very characters is capable of awakening spiritual images in the soul, and guiding us to what in our time the seer is to discover anew. This is the feeling the anthroposophist should cultivate on approaching this ancient record with which the Old Testament begins.

The Seven Days of Creation

Yesterday we painted a picture of the moments indicated by those meaningful words of the Bible: 'And God said, Let there be light: and there was light.' They allude to an event which portrays the recapitulation at a higher level of earlier evolutionary stages of our earth's development. I have to go on using the illustration of a human being who, on awakening, calls up from the depths of his soul a certain soul content. It is in some such way that what had slowly and gradually been built up during the course of the Saturn, Sun and Moon evolutions springs to life again in the soul of the elohim in a new, modified form. In fact all that is narrated in the Bible about the six or seven 'days' of creation is a reawakening of previous conditions, not in the same form but in one that was quite new. The next question we are permitted to ask is this: What kind of reality altogether are we to attribute to the account of what happened in the course of the six or seven 'days'?

It will be clearer if we put the question this way: Could an ordinary eye, in fact could any of our sense organs such as we have today have made rational sense of what we are told about the six days of creation? No, they could not. For the events being described there took place largely in the sphere we can call the realm of the elements, and a certain degree of clair-voyant perception would have been needed to observe them. The truth is that the Bible is telling us of the coming forth of sense existence out of the realms of the supersensible, and that the events of greatest significance are supersensible events, even if they are only one stage above our ordinary physical events which have proceeded from them. So in a certain respect, where all our descriptions of the six days of creation are concerned, we are in the domain of clairvoyant perception. What had existed at an earlier time now came forth in etheric or elemental form. We must get a firm grasp of this, otherwise we shall be all at sea regarding what the monumental words of Genesis really mean. So what we must expect to see is all that had evolved by stages during the Saturn, Sun and Moon evolutions emerging in a new form.

Let us begin, then, by asking what the conditions were actually like which pertained during the evolutions of these three planetary forms. On Saturn, as you can read up in my *Outline of Esoteric Science*, everything was in a kind of mineral condition. That which was there in the way of first rudiments of the human being, in fact the entire mass of ancient Saturn, was in a kind of mineral condition. However, this must not make you think of today's mineral form, for Saturn did not as yet have anything of the watery or solid elements in it; it was nothing but interweaving warmth. But the laws prevailing in this warmth planet, which brought differentiation about and brought order into the movement of the warmth, were the very same laws which govern the solid mineral kingdom. So when we say that both ancient Saturn and the human being were in a mineral condition, we must be aware that it was not like today's mineral condition, with its solid forms, but a state of weaving warmth governed by mineral laws.

Then came the Sun condition. We must think, here, of there still being no separation of the part which later became the earth. What today has become sun and earth was still in the form of one, unified body, a single cosmic body. In contrast to the earlier Saturn condition a coarsening took place, and a gaseous element arose, so that apart from the interweaving warmth we now have air streams intermingling and coming together in accordance with their own laws. But at the same time we have a new formation above it, a kind of rarefaction of warmth in the direction of light, a radiating of light into cosmic space. The actual nature of our planetary evolution progressed during the Sun period to the stage of the plant. Again we must not imagine that there were plants in their present form on old Sun; it is only that the same laws were at work there in the elements of warmth and air as rule in the plant kingdom today, those laws which determine that the root shall grow downwards and the blossom upwards. Obviously no solid plant forms could arise; we must think of the forces which send blossoms up and roots down, weaving in an airlike structure, and imagine the condition on ancient Sun as a lightlike flashing forth of blossoms in an upward direction. Picture a gaseous sphere and within it, living, weaving light which causes the gaseous vapour to shoot up in radiant blossoms, while at the same time below there is the effort to check these luminous outbursts and get the old Sun to hold together at its centre; then you have a picture of the inner weaving of light, warmth and air in the ancient Sun condition. The laws of the mineral kingdom are repeated and the laws of the plant kingdom are added, and the development of the human being as far as it has progressed is still only in a plantlike condition.

Where today would we find anything in the least comparable to this plantlike weaving in the air-warmth-light sphere of the Sun? With today's sense organs we would search the whole of cosmic space in vain. At a certain period of Sun evolution these conditions existed even physically—that is, as far as the density of air. Today they cannot exist physically at all. The form of activity which actually existed physically at that time can only be found today by directing the faculty of clairvoyant perception towards the region of the supersensible world where the archetypal beings are who belong to our materially physical plants, the entities whom we have come to know as the group souls of the plants. We know of course that behind the flora presenting itself to our physical senses there is something we call group souls. Nowadays they can only be found in spiritual realms by clairvoyant consciousness. These group souls of the plants are not present in the single plants such as we see growing out of the soil, but there is a group soul more or less for each species of plant, such as the rose, the violet, the oak and so on. In the spiritual realm there is not a spiritual being corresponding to each single plant, but we have to think of group souls for the various species. To the poverty-stricken, abstract thinking of today plant species are just abstract concepts. They were already so in the Middle Ages; and it was because even at that time people no longer knew of the living, spiritual activity that is the foundation of the physical world that the famous controversy arose between realism and nominalism—the dispute as to whether species were mere names or real spiritual entities. For clairvoyant consciousness this whole dispute is utter nonsense, for when it directs its attention to the plant covering of our earth it pierces through the external plant forms into a spiritual region where the group souls of the plants actually live as real beings. And these group souls are one and the same as what we call species. At the time when the air-warmth-light sphere of the Sun was at its full splendour, when the light, playing on the surface of the air, threw off the sparkling blossoms of the plants, these forms were the same, in the form of physical air, as the plant species which are only to be found today in spiritual realms. Let us keep firmly in mind that the plant 'types' which cover our earth today in the form of leafing and blossoming plants, trees and bushes pervaded the ancient Sun actually as group souls, as species.

At this point in evolution the human being had come so far that he was also in a plantlike condition. He was unable to awaken mental images within himself, to bring into a condition of consciousness what went on around him, anymore than today the plants can do so. The human being was himself in a plantlike condition, and his bodily form existed among those light forms in continuous up and down movement in the gaseous globe. The emergence in the cosmos of even the most primitive form of consciousness requires something very special. As long as our earth forces were still united with the Sun forces, as long, roughly speaking, as the Sun did not shine on to planet earth from outside, what we call consciousness could not come into being as part of the nature of earth; nor could an astral body, which is the basis of consciousness, enter into the physical and etheric body. For consciousness to arise a separation, a split had to happen, something had to split off from the sun. This is what happened during the third stage of our earth's evolution, during the ancient Moon epoch. When the Sun evolution had come to an end and had passed through a kind of cosmic night the whole structure appeared again, but now it had become sufficiently mature to appear as a duality. Everything of a sun nature split off as one cosmic body, and separate from the sun was the old Moon, upon which, now, there were only the elements of water, air and warmth. The old Moon was the earth of those times, and it was only because the beings living on it could receive the force of the sun from outside that they were able to take into themselves astral bodies and develop consciousness, i.e. reflect in inner experience what went on around them. Animal nature, therefore, a state of being that is inwardly alive and possesses consciousness, is dependent for its existence on a separation occurring between the life of the sun and the life of the earth. It was during the ancient Moon period that animal nature arose, and the human being in regard to his bodily nature had developed as far as the animal stage. There is more about this in my *Outline of Esoteric Science*.

So we see that the three conditions that preceded our earth, and are the pre-conditions for its development, are linked together by certain laws. On the Moon a fluid element was added to the gaseous element—a watery element on the one hand and sound on the other, a quality of sound, as I told you yesterday, which is a rarefaction of light. This is a rough description of evolution. What had taken place during those three conditions now re-emerged as the memory of the elohim; at first, as we saw yesterday, in a state of confusion, described in the Bible as *tohu wa'bohu*. The stream of forces which rayed from the centre to the periphery and from the periphery back again to the centre embraced at first the interactivity of all three elemental conditions—air, warmth and water. These were now undifferentiated, whereas previously the gaseous and the warmth elements on the old Sun, and the three forms, warmth, gas and water on the old Moon, had been differentiated. Now, during the *tohu wa'bohu* they were in motley confusion, flowing in and out of one another, so that in the early stages of earth development it was impossible to distinguish between water, air and warmth. They were all mixed together.

The first thing that happened next was that light burst into this confusion. And out of this soul/spiritual activity, which I have described as cosmic thinking, there arose a force which first of all separated the air of former times from the water of former times. I want to ask you to fix very clearly in your minds this moment following the coming of the light. If we were to put it into dry prose we would say: After the light had burst into the *tohu wa'bohu* the elohim divided the former air from the former water, so that it was possible to distinguish again between them. In the chaotic mass made up of all three elemental states, a separation came about into two distinct parts, one of which was of the nature of air, with the inclination to spread in all directions, and the other was of the nature of water, with the inclination to cohere and to draw together. But the two conditions were not at that time comparable to the air or water of today. The 'water' was very much thicker—and we shall soon see why. On the other hand, to get an idea of the constitution of the 'air' of that time, we cannot find a better comparison than if we look away from the earth and watch, up in the air, the watery element forming steamy vapour with a tendency to rise up in cloud form which falls again as rain; that is, it has an inclination to rise and an inclination to descend. Both belong to water, only the one aspect of water has the tendency to vapourize and to rise upwards as clouds and the other the tendency to pour down and assume a level surface. This is, of course, only a comparison, for what I am describing was occurring in an elemental condition.

If we want to characterize what happened further we have to say that the elohim, through their cosmic thinking, brought it about that a separation took place in the *tohu wa'bohu* between two elemental conditions. The one had the tendency to press upwards, to become vapour, that is, water transforming itself into air, whereas the other had the tendency to pour forth in a downward direction, that is, water becoming thicker and thicker as it coheres. These are the actual facts which are expressed in modern languages by saying for instance: 'The gods did something between the waters above and the waters below.' I have just described to you what the gods did. Within the 'waters' they brought it about that one element of it had the tendency to rise and the other the tendency to reach the centre. The something in between is not a description of anything tangible; it is just a way of saying that a separation has been brought about between the two forms of energy which I have just described. If you want a physical example, you could say that the elohim so acted on the waters that on the one side they rose up and had a tendency to form clouds and to spread out in space; and on the other side they had a tendency to accumulate upon the surface of the earth. In fact the separating was more in the realm of thought, and therefore the word in Genesis which expresses the separation must be so understood. The English authorized version of the Bible uses the word 'firmament' for this. The Hebrew word is *rakia*.[1] This word certainly does not mean anything which one can express in a physically material sense, but simply means the separating out of two directions of force.

This brings us to what is described in Genesis as the second 'day'. So if we wanted to translate it into our own language we should have to say that in the turbulance of the elements the elohim first divided the air from the water. This is quite an exact rendering of what is meant. The elohim divided what strove upwards, which of course includes a mixture of air and water, from what strove to contract into greater density. This is the second 'day' of creation.

Now we proceed to the next 'day'. What happens now? What has been sent forth and is spreading outwards and tending to form clouds has reached a condition which in a way is a recapitulation of an earlier condition; the condition, in a coarser form, of the ancient Sun stage. The element which tends towards contraction, which in a way repeats the densification to the stage of water of the ancient Moon, is now further differentiated, and this further separation constitutes what comes to pass on the third 'day' of creation. We can say that on the second 'day' the elohim separated the air from the water, whereas on the third 'day' they separate, within the element of water, what we know today as water from something which had not existed before, a new densification, the solid element. The solid element is there for the first time. At the Moon stage this solid, earthly element was not yet there. Now it is precipitated out of the watery element. Thus on the third 'day' of creation we have a process of condensation, and we have to say that, whereas on the second 'day' the elohim separated the air element from that of water, on the third 'day', within the old Moon substance, they separate the new water element from the earth element which now emerges as something completely new. Everything which I have hitherto described had already existed before, even if in another form. The first thing which is entirely new is the earth element, solid matter, which now appears on the third 'day'. This earth element, which has separated out from the water, is here for the first time. Not until now has the opportunity arisen for what was already there to show itself in renewed form.

What are the first things which take on form? Those forms which had already arisen on the old Sun, which we described as plants shooting up in the delicate airy element of the Sun—and which had then re-appeared on the old Moon in the watery element—though of course there were still no plants in the sense of today. It is only on the third 'day' that there is a recapitulation of this in the earth element itself. The plant realm is the first to be repeated in the earth element, and this is wonderfully described in the Bible. I will deal later with the question of how we should understand the 'days' of creation; for the moment, I am talking of the coming of the light and of the air, and of the separating of the water from solid matter. The solid element now brings forth from out of itself a recapitulation of plant nature. This is very graphically described in the Bible when it says that after the elohim had separated the earth from the water, plant life springs forth out of the earth. Thus the springing up of plant life on the so-called third 'day' is a recapitulation in the solid element of what already existed during the ancient Sun stage; a kind of cosmic memory. In the cosmic thinking of the elohim there now arose in a solid condition the plant life which had existed on the old Sun at the gaseous stage.

Everything is repeated in a different form. Plant life is in a condition in which plants are still not individualized as on our earth today. I therefore expressly drew attention to the fact that separate individual plants, such as we can see and touch in the external sense world today, were not in existence either during the old Sun stage or the old Moon stage, or even at the earth stage when plant life is recapitulated in the earth element. What *did* exist were the group souls of the plants, what we today call the kinds of plants or species, and which to clairvoyant consciousness are not abstractions but something existing in the spirit realm. These manifested in the supersensible realm as a recapitulation. And that is what the Bible tells us. It is a strange thing but biblical commentators hardly know what to make of the words 'And the earth brought forth grass and herb yielding seed after his kind.' We ought to say 'in the form of species', for this is the explanation. Plant life existed in the form of group souls, species; there were no individual plants such as there are today. You will misunderstand the whole description of the springing forth of plant life on the so-called third 'day' of creation unless you think of this group soul nature. You must understand clearly that there was no springing forth of plants in the present sense, but the forms of the species or the group soul nature of the plants sprang forth on a soul level from out of active cosmic thinking. So when on the third 'day' of creation we are told that the elohim separated out from the water the solid element, the fourth elemental condition, we find that in this 'solid' state—which of course in its original elemental form would not yet have been visible to the outer eye but only to clairvoyant sight—there was a re-appearance of the forms of the plant species.

There can not yet be a recapitulation of animal nature. We have already pointed out that animal nature could only make its appearance during the ancient Moon stage after a duality had come into being and the sun had begun to function from outside. Therefore a repetition of this process (the separation of the moon) had to occur before evolution could advance from the plant to the animal level. So we are told that after the third 'day' in the periphery of the earth an outer element of sun, moon and stars begin to take effect, that forces begin to work in from outside. Whereas we previously envisaged an activity coming forth from the planet itself, now, in addition to this, there was activity raying in from heavenly spaces. In other words, the actual process should be described roughly in the following way: In addition to the forces of the terrestrial globe itself, which could recapitulate on its own only as much as it had previously brought forth as a unity, the elohim, from out of their cosmic thinking, now brought forces into play which streamed down upon the planet from cosmic space. A cosmic dimension was added to the earthly dimension. For the present let us read nothing further into what is described on the so-called fourth 'day' of creation. What was brought about by this raying in of forces from outside? Those processes could now be repeated naturally which already existed during the old Moon stage—but only in an altered form. During the old Moon evolution those animals had come into being which could live in the elements of air and water. These could now begin to re-appear. Therefore Genesis tells us, in wonderful accord with the facts, how on the fifth 'day' the air and the water begin to teem with life. This is a recapitulation from out of the earth element of the old Moon evolution, but at a higher level and in a new form.

My dear friends, when we contemplate things such as this our anthroposophical striving turns into a tremendous reverence for these ancient documents. What is experienced by clairvoyant consciousness is recorded in this document in impressive words, in words full of power; it confirms for us what clairvoyance has already told us—that once the light has started to shed its rays from outside, the creatures which existed in the elements of air and water at the old Moon stage could re-appear. In face of such a soul-stirring discovery how can we attach any importance to intellectual criticisms of these things? What nonsense it makes of the argument that this document was written in primitive times when human knowledge was still at a childish level! A fine 'childish level', when we rediscover in these records the highest knowledge to which we can raise ourselves! Must we not ascribe to those who have given them to us the very spirituality which alone is able to reach to this revelation? Does not this document, bequeathed to us by those seers of old, bear witness to them? The contents of this document itself testify that its writers were inspired. Indeed, we need no historical proof, for the contents themselves are the only possible proof.

When we look at things this way we realize that it was only after the fifth 'day' of creation that anything new could happen. For everything which had to be repeated had already done so. Now the earth itself, which had emerged as a new element, could be populated by animal life and all the new forms arising from this. Therefore we find described in splendid realism how, on the sixth 'day' a new element appears whose existence is so to speak attached to the earth. The animals who are described as appearing in the world on the sixth 'day' are the ones who are bound to the earth, and who appear as a new element. So we see that until the fifth 'day' we have a recapitulation of what had gone before, but now at a higher stage and in a new form. On the sixth 'day', however, earth nature comes into its own for the first time and something is added which has only become possible because of earth conditions.

I have now so to speak given you a summary of the sixth 'day' of creation. I have shown you that the sages of old who brought their great wisdom of the six 'days' of creation into this hidden form must have been fully aware of the new element arising. And further, they must also have been fully aware that it was only within this earth element that the actual being of man could break in. We know that all that the human being went through during the old Saturn, Sun and Moon stages were preparatory stages for becoming man. We know that during the Saturn period the first rudiments of a human physical body were developed. During the Sun period the rudiments of an etheric or life body were added, and during the Moon period the rudiments of an astral body. What was repeated up to the end of the so-called fifth 'day' of creation contained an element of astrality. Everything which had being had astrality. To infuse the ego, the fourth member of human nature, into a being in this whole evolutionary complex was only possible when earth conditions had been fully created. So the elohim prepared the earth by recapitulating the earlier stages at a higher level throughout the five 'days' of creation. It was only then, because the recapitulation had taken a new form, that they had at their disposal a fitting vessel into which they could impress the human form, and this was the crowning of the whole of evolution.

If a mere recapitulation had followed, evolution as a whole would only have been able to advance to the animal stage, the astral level. But as, right from the beginning, with every repetition, an element was being poured in which finally revealed itself as the earth element, a vessel was finally arrived at into which the elohim could pour all that lived within them. I have already described what this was like—like having a group of seven people, each one of whom has learnt something different; they all have different capacities, but all are working towards the same goal. There is one particular thing they all want to do, and each one contributes what he does best. This leads to an achievement in common. No single individual has the strength to do it on his own, but together they have the strength. What could we say about seven people such as these, who create something in common? We could say that the product of their work bears the impress of the image they had made of their task. We must keep this in mind as an apt description of the way the seven elohim worked together to arrive finally at their crowning achievement: to pour human form into what could arise out of the repetition of earlier stages, because everything was given a new imprint. Suddenly, therefore, quite a new language is spoken in Genesis. Earlier on things are expressed in particular terms: 'the elohim created', 'the elohim spoke', and so on. We have the feeling we are dealing with something that was determined from the outset. Now, when the crowning of earth evolution is to appear, a new language is spoken: 'Let us . . .' and in the usual translation: 'Let us make man.' This sounds as if the seven were taking counsel together, as people do when they are endeavouring to fulfil a common task. Therefore, in what finally emerges as the crowning of the work of evolution, we have to see a product of the combined effort of all the elohim; that they all contribute, each as he is able, to this common task, and that the human etheric form ultimately appears as an expression of the capacities and strengths acquired by the elohim during the ancient Saturn, Sun and Moon stages.

In saying this we have indicated something of immense importance. We have so to speak touched on what can be called human dignity. In many an epoch of history the impression made upon religious minds, the feelings they felt by certain words, brought their consciousness far nearer to the truth than is the case today. The ancient Hebrew sages also knew these feelings, and when they turned their attention to the seven elohim it came over them that despite all their humility and reverence, the human being is a tremendously important part of the world if the differing activities of seven beings had to combine to bring him into existence. The human form on earth is a goal of the gods! When you feel the whole significance of these words you will realize that each one of us has a tremendous responsibility, an obligation to make the human form as perfect as possible. The possibility of perfection was given from the moment the elohim resolved to combine all their capacities for the achievement of the one goal. This is a divine heritage, and it has been entrusted to human beings to develop it to ever higher levels of perfection into far distant times. Our study of cosmic evolution in relation to the tremendous opening words of the Bible must, among other things, lead us in all humility and patience, but also with strength, to be feelingly aware of this goal. These words not only disclose our origin but also point to our goal and highest ideal. We feel ourselves to be of divine origin, but we feel, too, what I tried to show in my Rosicrucian drama, at the point where the initiate reaches a certain stage and feels himself to be at the level of 'O Man, experience thyself!'[2] He is well aware of his human weakness, but also of his divine goal. He will no longer pass away, no longer become dried up in soul, but he feels uplifted, feels he is being inwardly experienced when he experiences himself, when he is able to experience himself in his other self that is filled with something that is akin to his own soul because it is his own divine goal.

The Forming and Creating of Beings by the Elohim. The Aeons or Time Spirits

We have pointed out that in the Genesis account of the coming into being of earth there is first of all a recapitulation of those earlier stages of evolution which can only be reached today through clairvoyant investigation, which is what we recognize as the source of our anthroposophical world outlook. If we recall what we have learnt about the conditions of evolution in periods prior to the existence of our earth circumstances, we can picture that what later became our solar system was all contained in a planetary existence which we call ancient Saturn; and we keep very firmly in mind that ancient Saturn consisted solely of the interweaving movement of warmth. If anyone from the standpoint of modern physics wants to raise any objections to my speaking of a cosmic body consisting solely of warmth, I must refer him to what I said two days ago—that I myself could raise all the objections of so-called science against the things said here today or at any other time. But there is really not the time in these lectures to touch on what this gullible modern science has to say. Compared with the sources of spiritual scientific investigation the whole range of what has come from modern scientific knowledge seems pretty amateurish. I intend one day to deal with some of the objections raised, probably beginning next spring at the time of my lectures in Prague when I shall be speaking not only about the whole basis of anthroposophy but, in order to satisfy contemporary minds, also about the arguments against it.[1] Therefore my Prague lectures will be preceded by two public lectures of which the first will be entitled: How can anthroposophy be refuted? And the second: How can anthroposophy be substantiated?

Later on I shall repeat these lectures in other places, and people will then see that we ourselves are fully aware of the objections which can be made against what is taught in anthroposophy, and can say it all ourselves. Anthroposophy has a firm foundation, and those who think they are able to refute it do not yet understand it. This will be adequately shown in the course of time. As to Saturn's state of warmth, let me once more draw attention to several observations in my book *An Outline of Esoteric Science*, which may even help to satisfy those who are prompted by their scientific training to make objections.

Having said this I feel free to resume speaking about anthroposophy without further reference to objections, even the well-meant ones.

In ancient Saturn, then, there was an interweaving of varying states of warmth. Let us visualize this very clearly. According to Genesis there is a repetition within the developing earth of this ancient Saturn state, this interweaving of warmth or fire. This is the first thing in the development of the elements that we want to picture. But note well in what way we speak of warmth or fire in connection with such an exalted condition as that of ancient Saturn. We shall not get anywhere near it by striking a match or lighting a candle and examining fire or warmth from a physical point of view. We have to think of what we are here calling warmth or fire as something much more spiritual, or more exactly as something of the nature of soul. Feel yourself as a warmth-bearing being—and this feeling of your own warmth, this experience of your own soul warmth, will give you a rough idea of the interweaving warmth in ancient Saturn.

Then we press forward to the second evolutionary condition of our planet, to ancient Sun, and speak of how, in the development of the elements, warmth has condensed to what we call a gaseous or aeriform state. Here we have to differentiate between warmth on the one hand and gas or air on the other. However, we have already referred to the fact that alongside the condensation of warmth into air, that is to say, with the descent of the elemental state into something coarser, there is an ascent to something more rarefied, more of an etheric nature. So if we call the elemental condition below warmth 'air', we have to call the next one above warmth 'light', light ether. If we then look at the elemental conditions all together during the Sun evolution, we should say that in ancient Sun there was an intermingling of warmth, light and air, and all life at that time clothed itself in the elements of warmth, light and air. We must realize once again that if we direct our attention only to these elemental manifestations of warmth, light and air we are only so to speak seeing the outer aspect—the *maya*, the illusion—of what is really there. In reality these are spiritual beings manifesting themselves outwardly by means of warmth, light and air. It is somewhat as if we were to put a hand into a heated room and say to ourselves: The reason why this room is warm is because there is a being in there who is giving out warmth, and for whom this spreading of warmth is a means of manifestation.

If we now advance to ancient Moon, there again we have warmth as the middle condition and below it a consolidation into air or gas and below that a consolidation into water. Light appears again, and then, above light so to speak, what is a finer, more etheric state. I have already said that we may give the name 'sound ether' to this force which works within substances as an organizing principle, combining them and splitting them apart. We could also call it 'numerical ether', because it is this spiritual sound which arranges all material existence according to measure and number. Human beings only recognize this force with their outer senses when it is transmitted by the air, yet spiritually it is at the foundation of all existence. So even though we say we ascend from light to sound we must not confuse it with external sound conveyed by the air, but recognize it as something that is only perceptible when the clairvoyant sense is awake to it. Both in old Moon itself, therefore, and in all that works upon it from outside, we see the elemental conditions of warmth, air, water, light and sound.

When we advance to the fourth stage, the coming into being of the actual earth, a further level of condensation and a further level of rarefaction are added—the earthy or solid condition below, and what we call 'life ether' above, which is a still finer ether than sound ether. So we may describe the elemental consistency of the earth by saying that warmth is again the middle condition, the denser ones being air, water and solid matter, and the rarefied ones light, sound and life ether. To make sure that there is no risk at all of anything remaining unclear, I will explicitly state once again that what is described as earth or solid matter must not be confused with what modern science calls earth. What is being described here is something which is not directly visible around us. In an occult sense what we stand on when we stand on the ground is of course earth in so far as it is solid, but gold, silver, copper and tin are also earth. Everything of a solid/material nature is earth from the occult point of view. The modern physicist will of course say that this distinction means nothing. 'Let us distinguish our various elements, but we know nothing about a kind of archetypal earthly substance that is meant to be the basis of these elements.' Only when the clairvoyant eye penetrates the external elements—some seventy of them— and searches for the foundation of solid matter, for the forces that make matter into the solid state, does he discover, behind sense existence, the very forces which, in the occult sense, form, shape and put together the solid, fluid and gaseous elements. This is what we are talking about. And this is also what Genesis is talking about, if we really understand it. According to Genesis, then, we shall expect to find that of these four conditions the first three are bound to repeat in some fashion, but that the fourth appears as something new in earth existence.

On the strength of this let us test Genesis accordingly, and let us do so with the same methods we adopted for the earlier lectures. In the coming into being of our earth we should expect to find a repetition of the old Saturn condition. In other words we should expect to find Saturn warmth as the expression of soul/spiritual forces. And this is just what we do find if we really understand Genesis. I told you that the words that are usually translated as 'And the spirit of God moved upon the face of the waters' really mean that the soul/spiritual essence of the elohim spreads out and that this very element of warmth—the kind of warmth we think of as radiating down from the hen into the eggs in the process of brooding—enters into the elements that were there at the time. With the words 'The spirit of God radiated as a brooding warmth over the elements or the water' you have an indication of the recapitulation of the warmth of ancient Saturn.

Let us go on. The next condition ought to be one that represents a recapitulation of ancient Sun. For the time being let us ignore the condensation process which proceeded from warmth to air, and only look at the process of rarefaction, the element of light. Let us pinpoint the fact that during the Sun period the light invaded cosmic space, then the recapitulation of the old Sun evolution in earth's development will be the coming of the light. This is announced in the mighty words: 'And God said, Let there be light! and there was light.'

The third recapitulation ought to be that in the series of the more rarefied elemental conditions what we call the organizing sound ether streams into earth development. So let us ask ourselves whether there is in fact any indication of such a recapitulation of the Moon evolution in Genesis. What would we expect to find? We would expect sound to set to work to organize elemental conditions more or less in the way we see Chladni's sound forms arising when a violin bow is drawn down the edge of a metal plate covered with fine dust. There would have to be a recapitulation which would tell us that sound ether sets to work and organizes matter in some way. What, then, are we actually told about the moment of creation which followed the coming of the light? We are told that the elohim stirred up the masses of elemental substance so that a change came about in the way they were arranged, and some of them streamed upwards and some of them collected together below. A force entered into the elemental masses and altered the way they were arranged, just as sound takes hold of the dust and brings about the Chladni sound figures. In the same way as the dust moves into different places and forms a pattern, the elemental masses moved, and some streamed upwards, and some gathered together below. The word *rakia*, which is used to describe what the elohim introduced into the elemental masses, is difficult to translate, and the usual translations are inadequate to render it correctly. Even when one takes into account all that can be contributed today towards its elucidation, including what philology has to say, one has to admit that neither the translation 'firmament' nor any of its variants takes us very far. For there is something active, something rousing about it. A more precise philology would find that this word contains the very thing I am pointing to here—that the elohim stirred up something in the elemental masses which may be compared to what is set going among the dust particles of the Chladni sound figures when the sound alters the pattern. In the same way as the dust particles move into a different arrangement, the elemental masses move either upwards or downwards on the second 'day' of creation. So we see in Genesis the coming of sound ether following on after light ether. In absolute accordance with the facts of the second 'day' of creation, this presents us with what from a certain aspect is a recapitulation of Moon evolution.

You will readily see of course that these recapitulations cannot happen in an entirely unequivocal manner but that, as it were, they overlap. So the apparent contradiction between today's exposition and that of yesterday will easily be cleared up. The recapitulations take place in such a way that first there occurs what I am now telling you and then there is a more comprehensive recapitulation, as I described yesterday.

After the moment in the coming into being of the earth when sound ether has brought about a change in the elements to the point where some rise upwards and the others accumulate below, we ought to expect to find something becoming active which we have described as the rarefied substance of the earth, and have called life, life ether. Something can be expected to follow on after the second 'day' of the creation which would indicate that life ether was pouring into the elemental masses of our earth just as previously light and organizing sound ether had poured in. There should be some phrase in Genesis to indicate that life ether burst in and brought about the stirring and unfolding of life. Look at the Genesis account of the third 'day' of creation. We are told that the earth brings forth green and living things, herbaceous plants and trees according to their kind. Here is a vivid description of the pouring in of life ether, calling forth everything that is said to have come into being on the third 'day'.

Thus we find in Genesis all that occultism can bring to light through clairvoyant investigation and that we should expect to find if Genesis itself really derives from occult knowledge. It confirms it, if we have the will to understand it. It is a wonderful experience, after we have first done our research independently of any document, to find it confirmed in Genesis. I can assure you that when, in my *Outline of Esoteric Science*, I was describing the way the earth came into existence as a recapitulation of ancient Saturn, ancient Sun and ancient Moon, I quite deliberately and scrupulously ignored anything which could have been found in Genesis. I only presented what I was able to discover independently of any external document. But if you then compare these independent findings with Genesis you see that the latter presents us with a document which says just what our independent research has enabled us to say. This is the wonderful harmony I pointed to yesterday, where what we can say of our own accord comes sounding back to us, as it were, through the spiritual faculties of seers who spoke to us millennia ago.

Thus in the first three 'days' of creation we see as regards the more rarefied elements of our earth a successive activity of warmth, light, sound ether and life ether and in what these activities stir up and enliven we see at the same time the unfolding of stages of densification—from warmth to air, then to water and finally to solid matter, to the earth element, in the way I have described. The processes of densification and of rarefaction interpenetrate one another, and together they give us a unified picture of the coming into existence of the earth. Whether we speak of the denser conditions—air, water, earth—or of the more rarefied states—light ether, sound ether and life ether—we are concerned with manifestations, with the outer garments of soul/spiritual beings. From the Genesis point of view, the first of these soul/spiritual beings to appear before the mind's eye are the elohim, and from an anthroposophical point of view we feel bound to ask: What kind of beings are the elohim? So that we may know where we are we must be able to give them their proper place in the order of the hierarchies. You will no doubt remember from the various lectures I have given over the years, or from what you have read in my *Outline of Esoteric Science*, that in the hierarchical order, when we begin at the top, we can distinguish first a trinity which we call seraphim, cherubim and thrones. You know that we then recognize a second trinity which we call kyriotetes or dominions, the dynamis or mights, and the exusiai or powers, revelations; when we come to the lowest trinity, using Christian designations we call them archai or beginnings, principalities or spirits of personality, archangels or archangeloi, and angels or angeloi; those in this lowest group being the spiritual beings who are nearest to man. Only then do we come in the order of the hierarchies to man himself as the tenth member within our hierarchical order. Now the question is, where, among the angelic hosts, do the elohim belong?

If we look at the second of the trinities, at those beings we call exusiai or powers or spirits of form, this is the position the elohim have. We know from what has been presented over the years that during the ancient Saturn evolution the archai, the spirits of personality, were at the human stage, the stage which we are at now. During the ancient Sun evolution the archangels were at the human stage, during the ancient Moon evolution the angels, and during earth evolution it is man who is at this stage. The spirits of form, the exusiai, the ones we call the elohim, are one level above the spirits of personality. Thus they are lofty spiritual beings who had already advanced beyond the human stage when our planetary existence began on ancient Saturn. We get an idea of the sublimity of these beings when we realize that in the order of the hierarchies they are four stages above the human level. The force which was at work there, the force active in cosmic thinking which brought earth existence into being is, in the ranks of the hierarchies, four stages higher than man. Human beings can work creatively only in their thought forms, whereas because the thinking of the elohim is four stages higher than human thinking it can not only shape, form and create within the world of thought but can do so within the realm of being.

Having been told this you are bound to ask: What about the other beings of the hierarchies? First, we should like to know what part those beings play in Genesis whom we have just named as the archai or spirits of personality. They are, as we see, the next rank down in the hierarchical order. Let us remind ourselves again that the elohim are highly exalted beings who, at the time of the ancient Saturn evolution, had already progressed beyond the human stage. They were among the beings creating and regulating evolution during the stages of ancient Saturn, Sun and Moon, and they also contributed to earth existence. Compared with this, what can we expect of the hierarchy which is immediately below that of the elohim, namely the spirits of personality? Does Genesis not tell us anything about them? Since we know from Genesis what lofty beings the elohim are, we actually should expect these principalities or spirits of personality to be engaged in serving them, so to speak. After the elohim had performed their mighty deeds of creation does Genesis say anything to the effect that they relegated the lesser activities to their servants the archai or beginnings? The elohim performed the chief, most comprehensive tasks, but after they had carried out the broad sweeps, had displayed their tremendous creative powers, did they not for instance leave the archai or spirits of personality to deputize for them?

To answer the question as to whether Genesis says anything about the elohim availing themselves of beings such as those who were below them in rank, and setting them to deputize for them, we have to discover what Genesis is really saying. There is a subject in Genesis which has been a veritable stumbling block to materialistic commentators because for centuries these Bible commentators have completely ignored what occult research has to say about the actual meaning of the opening words of our Bible. If you are at all familiar with Bible criticism you will know what difficulty this point has caused. There is a sentence in Genesis which is rendered: 'And God divided the light from the darkness' and we are then told that light and darkness alternate. I shall come back to a closer examination of these words. For the moment I will make use of the modern version. It is not right, of course, and is only being used for the time being. At a particular place it says: 'And the evening and the morning were the first day.' And then it says: 'And God called the light day.' This is a real stumbling block for the scholars! What then is a 'day' of creation? The naïve mind regards a day as lasting twenty-four hours and alternating between light and darkness as do the kind of days during which we go through a waking and a sleeping period. You all know of course how much scorn has been heaped on this naïve notion of the world being created in seven ordinary days. You may also know how much trouble— you could say fruitless trouble—has been spent trying to identify the days of creation with longer or shorter periods, or as geological periods and so on, so that a 'day' of creation could signify a longer period of time.

The first difficulty arises of course when we come to the fourth 'day', when Genesis first speaks of the setting up of the sun and the moon to direct time. Every child today knows that the regulating of our twenty-four hour day depends on the relationship of the earth to the sun. But if this relationship was not set up until the fourth 'day' we cannot speak of that kind of day before that. So anyone who tries to adhere to the naïve belief that we are dealing in Genesis with days of twenty-four hours would be transgressing against Genesis itself. There may be such people of course, but they have to be told that by insisting that Genesis refers to days such as ours they are certainly not supported by revelation. As to the vagaries of those who try to find a way out by giving geological meaning to these 'days' of creation, they are really not worth bothering about. For in the whole range of literature on the subject there is not the slightest evidence that the word *yom* signifies anything resembling a geological period.[2] So it is a very real question for us: What does this word *yom* mean, which is usually translated as 'day'?

Only those people can form a judgement about this who are able to transport themselves with their whole feeling into ancient methods of naming things. To do this you have to have quite a different kind of feeling and sensitivity than we have today. So as not to put you in too much of a quandary let us take it step by step. Firstly let me draw your attention to an ancient doctrine held by the gnostics. They spoke of spiritual powers who played a part in our existence, entering successively into evolution, and they called these powers, these entities, aeons. When people spoke of aeons in a gnostic sense they did not mean periods of time but beings. What is meant is that a first aeon acts, and having executed the work of which he is capable, is succeeded by a second aeon; and after the second has exhausted his capacities a third takes over, and so on. When the gnostics spoke of aeons they meant beings guiding evolution in succession, one taking over from another. It was only very much later that the purely abstract concept of time was associated with the word 'aeon'. Aeon is a being, a living entity. And in the same sense as 'aeon' is a living entity, so is the Hebrew word *yom*. It has nothing to do with a merely abstract designation of time, but is a living being. So when we are told about seven such *yamim* following one another, we are dealing with seven consecutive beings or groups of beings.

We find the same thing elsewhere concealed in a verbal resemblance. In the more Aryan languages there is a connection between *deus* and *dies*—'God' and 'day'. There is an essential inner relationship. In earlier times the connection between day and being was clearly felt, and when people spoke of days of the week as we speak of Sunday, Monday, Tuesday and so on, they did not simply mean periods of time but the groups of beings active in sun, moon, mars and so on. Once we accept the word *yom* as a spiritual being instead of in its usual rendering as 'day' then we have the hierarchical beings one stage lower than the elohim, beings of whom the elohim avail themselves as subordinate beings. After the elohim, with their superior powers of organizing, had actively brought light into existence, they then put in charge of it, according to Genesis, *yom*, the first of the time spirits, or archai. Thus the spiritual beings whom we call spirits of personality or principalities are the same as those called periods of time, 'days', *yamim*. They are the servants of the elohim, who execute as it were what the elohim dispose from their higher vantage point. Those of you who heard the lectures I gave recently in Christiana will remember that there too I called the archai 'time spirits', and described the way they still work as time spirits today.[3] These were the servants of the elohim, and they appointed them so to speak to carry out the plans of which they themselves had prepared the broad outlines. Even as far as our understanding reaches, everything fits together in one large system. But, of course, only when you have followed up over years what is being said, will you acquire a real grasp of the way everything fits completely into place.

So we can say that as beings on an exalted level the elohim intervened in the interweaving ethers of air, water and earth, and appointed beings below them in rank as their servants, if we may use this everyday expression. They so to speak gave them orders. When they had poured light into existence they transferred to these beings the elaboration of what they had set going. Therefore we may say that after the elohim had created the light they put in charge of it the first of the time spirits in their service. It is this spirit who is concealed behind the customary words 'the first day'. We shall of course only understand the still deeper meaning of what is meant by 'the first day' when we also understand the rest of the statement: 'And the evening and the morning were the first day.' It means that the first of the time spirits became active and associated with this what can be described as an alternation between *erev* and *boker*.[4] *Erev* is not the same as evening nor *boker* the same as morning. An appropriate translation would be: 'And *erev* came about—a state of confusion—and *boker*—a state of order.' We should say: 'And a state of disorder appeared followed by a state of order, of harmony, within which the first of the time spirits was active.'

SATURN	SUN	MOON	EARTH
			life
		sound	sound
	light	light	light
warmth (*fire*)	warmth	warmth	warmth
	air	air	air
		water	water
			earth

Lecture 5, 21 August 1910

Light and Darkness, Yom and Laila

If we look back once more at what we have learnt about our earth's beginnings we find many things which still need to be explained. The investigations we have made so far show us that there is far more in the way of living beings to be found in the verbal descriptions of Genesis than is seen from the usual Bible translations.

Yesterday we pointed out that the word *yom*, 'day', is not the abstract division of time which at present we call day, but refers to the beings whom we call spirits of personality, time spirits or archai in the hierarchical order. This discovery persuades us to enter even more deeply into what I have already said many times, namely that behind the weaving life of elemental existence described in Genesis soul/spiritual beings are to be found everywhere. Therefore, if we pursue the matter we may discover beings instead of empty abstractions behind some of the other things we are looking at in Genesis. Of course it is easy to see the existence of beings when we hear: the spirit of the elohim, *ruach elohim*.[1] But if we want to arrive at the real meaning of the old records we have to look for beings not only in those expressions, where probably even modern minds would be prepared to see them, but track them down wherever they are. So we should be justified in asking what is concealed for instance behind the expression, put now in my own words: 'And the inner activity was *tohu wa'bohu*, and darkness was upon the material existence of the elements.' Do we not possibly have to see some kind of being behind what is described as 'darkness'? We cannot understand Genesis at all unless we can answer such questions. Just as we have to see all the positive elements such as light, air, water, earth and warmth solely as the manifestations of spiritual beings, perhaps we should also see in the more negative expressions solely the outer manifestation of some being hidden more deeply behind them?

To get to the bottom of this we must go back to the earliest point we can reach in the development of our planet. As we have often said, we must think of the ancient Saturn existence as a condition of pure warmth, and that with the transition to the ancient Sun existence there then took place a densification to air and gas, and on the other hand a rarefaction in the direction of the etheric, to light ether. We therefore understand the passage 'And God (the elohim) said, Let there be light, and there was light' to be a kind of repetition of the coming of this etheric light.

We may ask: Was the darkness there of itself, or is there also a being hidden behind this? If you read the relevant chapter in my *Outline of Esoteric Science* something will occur to you which is extremely important for the understanding of all development—the fact that at each stage of evolution certain beings remain behind. Only a certain number of beings reach their goal. I have often used a superficial but drastic expression, and pointed out that not only do some school children worry their parents by having to remain another year in the same class, but that in the cosmic process, too, certain beings actually remain behind at a previous stage and do not attain their required level. So we may say that during the ancient Saturn evolution certain beings did not reach their proper goal but lagged behind, and during the ancient Sun evolution they were still at the Saturn stage.

How would one recognize, during the ancient Sun existence, beings who were still Saturn beings? By the fact that they had not reached the level of being of ancient Sun which was of the nature of light. But because these Saturn beings were nevertheless there, the Sun condition, which I have described as an interweaving of light, warmth and air, had darkness interspersed in the light. This darkness was the expression of the beings remaining at the Saturn stage just as much as the weaving light was the expression of those beings who had reached the Sun stage in a regular way. The outer aspect showed a manifestation of the interweaving of retarded Saturn beings with Sun beings who had progressed normally. From the inner aspect these beings moved in and out among one another, and outwardly they manifested as an interplay of light and darkness. Looking at the light we can call it a manifestation of the beings who had progressed to the Sun stage, and looking at the darkness we can call it the external manifestation of the beings who had remained behind at the Saturn stage.

Once we realize this we can expect to find that during the recapitulation of ancient Saturn and ancient Sun on planet earth the relationship between the advanced and the retarded beings will re-appear. And because the retarded Saturn beings represent an earlier stage of evolution, so to speak, they will be able, during the recapitulation too, to appear sooner than the light. Thus, quite rightly, in the first verse of Genesis we are told that the darkness prevailed over the elemental masses. This is the recapitulation of the Saturn condition, but it was the retarded Saturn condition. The other one, the Sun condition, has to wait. It comes later on, at the point where the Bible says: 'Let there be light.' Thus we see in a most pertinent way that with regard to these recapitulations, too, Genesis gets it just right.

If we really want to understand existence we must be clear about the fact that what has emerged at a previous stage did not just persist for a while and then fade away. On the contrary, the truth is that although something new is continually arising the older element remains alongside the new one and continues to function within it. Thus even today the two stages of evolution, which we can call the relationship between light and darkness, still co-exist on earth. Light/darkness is really something that is interwoven into our existence. However, as far as present times are concerned this is a very thorny subject indeed.

I do not know whether any of you are aware that for the past thirty years or so I have repeatedly been trying to demonstrate how very significant and valuable Goethe's *Theory of Colour* is.[2] Of course, anyone who stands up for it today must be quite clear about the fact that he will not gain the ear of his contemporaries. For those whose knowledge of physics would qualify them to understand what one is talking about with regard to Goethe's colour theory are far too immature to get any idea of the essence of it. Modern physics, with its fantastic nonsense about ether vibrations and so on, is utterly incapable of penetrating to the core of Goethe's colour theory. For this we shall have to wait a few more decades. Anyone who deals with the subject knows that. And the others—forgive me for saying this—who are in the occult direction mature enough to understand the essential nature of Goethe's colour theory know far too little about physics for me to be able to go into the matter properly. So the foundation for it is still not there. For what is at the heart and core of Goethe's colour theory is the mystery of the interaction of light and darkness as two polar opposite spiritual entities in the world. The fantastic notion put forward today as the theory of matter which, in the manner in which people think of it today is an illusion and has no existence at all—this concept of matter is a soul/spiritual being concealed behind all the instances where the polarity of light and darkness is operating. What physicists today call the concept of matter is in fact fantasy. In the regions of space where according to physics we are to look for a sort of apparition called 'matter', there is in fact nothing else but a certain degree of darkness. This dark volume of space is filled with soul/spiritual being that has an affinity to something certainly mentioned in Genesis where all these soul/spiritual beings are described as darkness, and we are told that this darkness surges over elemental existence. All these things are much more profound than modern science would dream of. Thus when Genesis speaks of darkness it is speaking of the manifestation of the backward Saturn beings, and when it speaks of light it is referring to the manifestation of the advanced beings. They interact and interweave with one another.

We said yesterday that the main features of evolution were laid down by those beings whom we have placed at the same level as the exusiai, the spirits of form, so it is these beings who plan the overall activities of the light. And further, we have seen that they use the spirits of personality as their servants, and that behind the expression *yom*, 'day', we have to see a being of the rank of the archai, one appointed by the elohim. So we may also assume that, just as these servants of the elohim, these spirits of personality called *yom*, 'day', are active in the positive direction, there are, as opposed to them, backward spiritual beings active in darkness. We can also say that whereas darkness is something the elohim find already in existence, they produce light through their creative thinking. When, from what has remained of ancient existence, they think out the two complexes of thoughts, it transpires that the darkness interwoven in it is the expression of the retarded beings. They themselves contribute the light. But just as out of the light the elohim appoint the beings called *yom*, 'day', so out of the darkness come beings who are of the same rank as these, but beings who have lagged behind at an earlier stage. So we can say that all that manifests as darkness is a common front in opposition to the elohim. We therefore have to ask:

Who are the beings who oppose the servants of the light, the archai, the beings indicated by the term *yom*? Who are the corresponding backward beings in opposition to them?

To avoid misunderstanding, it would be a good thing if we were first to answer another question, namely whether we have always to think of retarded beings as evil, as something wrong in the world context. An abstract person, someone who only sticks to concepts, can easily become almost indignant about the backward beings, or he can go the other way and feel sorry for the poor things! We should not allow ourselves to have any feelings and ideas of this kind when it comes to cosmic realities of this dimension and significance. That would be quite wrong. On the contrary, we have to realize that whether beings attain their goal or whether they stop at an earlier stage of evolution, all these things happen from out of cosmic wisdom, and that whenever beings remain behind at a particular stage, it means something. It means just as much to evolution as a whole whether beings remain behind or whether they attain their goal; in other words, there are certain functions which cannot be carried out at all by the progressive beings, and for these functions beings are needed who remain behind at an earlier stage. Their backwardness puts them in exactly the right place. We could well ask: What would become of the world if all the people who ought to be teachers of young children became university professors? Those who do not become professors are much better where they are than the more learned ones would be. The university professors would probably be most unsuitable teachers for children from the ages of six to ten. It is the same in cosmic relationships. There are certain tasks for which those who attain their goal would be not at all fitted. For these tasks those who have remained behind—we could equally well say those who have renounced progress—must take their place. And just as the advanced spirits of personality, the *yamim*, were put in their places by the elohim, the retarded archai too, those spirits of personality who manifest not through light but through darkness, are made use of so that the whole course of earth's becoming should progress with well-ordered harmony. They are allotted their right place so that they may make their proper contribution to the regular development of our existence.

How important this is we can see from an illustration taken from everyday life. The light spoken of in Genesis is not the light we can see with our physical eyes, which is a later expression of it. Similarly, what we designate as physical darkness, which surrounds us at night when the sun is not shining, is a later physical form of what is called darkness in Genesis. If we were to ask whether the kind of physical daylight we see today has a certain significance for human beings, none of you would doubt that it has, both with regard to human beings and with regard to other creatures. Take for example the plants, which wither if they are removed from the light. Light is an element of life for every living thing, so it is also essential for human beings as far as their external bodily existence is concerned.

But something else is necessary apart from light. To understand what this is we have to turn our attention to the effect the alternation between waking and sleeping has on our physical and etheric bodies. What does it really mean to be awake? What are we human beings doing when we are awake? Basically, the whole of our soul activity, all that goes on in the realms of our mental images and our feelings, all the ebb and flow of our passions—in short, all that takes place within the surging activity of our astral body and our ego—constitutes a continual wearing down of our physical body during the daytime. This is a very ancient occult truth, one which even our current physiology arrives at if it only knows how to interpret its own findings properly. The activity taking place in our inner soul life when we are awake is continuously using up the forces of the external physical body, the first rudiments of which we acquired during ancient Saturn. The life of the physical body is quite different during sleep when the astral body with its fluctuating inner life is outside it. Just as in waking life there is a continuous using up, we could even say destroying of the forces of the physical body, in sleep these forces are constantly being restored and regenerated. So that in our physical and etheric bodies we have to distinguish two different processes at work: destructive processes taking place during waking life and processes of renewal taking place during sleep. But nothing that happens in the world of space leads an isolated life of its own; all is connected with existence as a whole. So when we focus on the destructive processes taking place in our physical body from the time we wake up until we go to sleep again, we must not regard them as though they occurred in isolation within the confines of our skin, but realize that they are intimately connected with cosmic processes. They are a continuation of what flows into us from outside; so that during waking life we are connected with the destructive forces of the universe and during sleep with the forces of regeneration.

This decomposition process of our physical body going on during our waking day could not have happened during ancient Saturn, otherwise the first rudiments of our physical body could not possibly have been formed. For obviously you cannot build up anything if you then start to destroy it. The activity on Saturn with regard to the physical body had to be a constructive one, and that was what was being taken care of on Saturn. The destructive processes in our body take place particularly in the daytime, under the influence of the light, but there was as yet no light during ancient Saturn. This is why the work of Saturn on our physical body was an up-building one. For a time, at least, this up-building activity had to be maintained, even when, later on during the ancient Sun existence the light was added, and this could only happen because Saturn beings who had remained behind were there to take care of it. So you see how necessary it was for the Saturn beings to be kept back in cosmic evolution, so that they could undertake the rebuilding of the worn down physical body during sleep while there was no light. The retarded Saturn beings have to be a part of our existence. Without them we should be exposed to nothing but destruction. There has to be an alternation, an interaction between Sun and Saturn beings, between the beings of light and the beings of darkness. Therefore if the activity of the light beings was to be rightly guided by the elohim these light beings had to introduce into their work a right and proper interweaving of the work of the beings of darkness. There is no possibility of stability in cosmic activity unless the force of darkness is always being interwoven with the force of light. And this kind of network of the forces of light and of darkness is one of the mysteries of cosmic existence, of cosmic alchemy. This mystery is touched upon in the seventh scene of my first Mystery Play where Johannes Thomasius enters devachan and where one of Maria's companions, Astrid, is given the task of weaving the dark into the light.[3] Throughout the conversation between Maria and her three companions you will find many cosmic mysteries concealed which can well be pondered on for a long, long time.

Thus we must never forget that we have to regard this interplay between the forces of the light of the sun and the darkness of Saturn as a necessity of our existence. When therefore the elohim placed the spirits of personality as their deputies, in charge of the weaving of the light forces, of the work which is being performed upon us human beings or upon earthly creatures altogether under the influence of the light, they had to appoint the backward Saturn beings to be their companions. The total activity of the cosmos had to be a confluence of the interworking of the archai who had progressed normally and the backward ones. These backward archai are active in the darkness. To put it simply the elohim employ not only those beings called *yom* but set against them the beings who work in darkness. And the Bible gives a wonderfully realistic description of the facts when it says: 'And God called the light "day" (*yom*) and the darkness he called "night" (*laila*).'[4] This is not our abstract night, these are the Saturn archai who at that time had not advanced to the Sun stage. To this day it is they who are active in us during sleep when they exert their influence to build up our physical and etheric bodies. This mysterious expression *laila*, which has given rise to all kinds of myths, is neither our abstract 'night' nor is it anything which could lead us to think of mythology. It is simply the name of the backward archai, of those beings who unite their work with that of the advanced archai.

Thus we have paraphrased the respective passages in Genesis as follows: The elohim planned the main outlines of existence and appointed to the subordinate posts the progressive archai and gave them as helpers those archai who in resignation had remained in darkness at the Saturn stage, in order that existence could come about. So we have *yom* and *laila* as the two opposite groups of beings who are the helpers of the elohim, and who are at the level of time spirits, of spirits of personality. We see existence being woven out of the spirits of form and the spirits of personality, out of advanced beings and backward beings of these two respective stages.

If we have found more or less satisfying answers to what is being presented here (there is infinitely more behind all these things), another question could present itself now, which is bound to be on the tip of all your tongues. What of the other hierarchies? If we descend from the spirits of form we come first to the archai, the spirits of personality, then to the arch-angels, archangeloi, spirits of fire. Does Genesis say nothing at all about them? Let us look more closely and find out what the actual position is with regard to these fire spirits. We know that they reached their human stage during the Sun evolution. Then they progressed further through the Moon stage to that of earth. They are beings who are intimately connected with everything we can call sun nature, for it was during the Sun evolution that they reached their human stage. And when, during the ancient Moon evolution, it became necessary for the sun to separate from the earth, which was at that time of a moon nature, then these beings, who had gone through their most important stage on the Sun, and who were by their very nature associated with the Sun, naturally remained united with the Sun. When therefore the Moon (later to become earth) separated from the Sun, these beings remained not with the separating earth/moon but with the Sun. These are the beings who work upon the earth chiefly from outside.

I have already mentioned to you that in the evolution from Saturn to Sun the highest form of life which could arise on the Sun was the plant species. Animal nature, a species which has inner life, could arise only in conjunction with a separation; therefore it was not until the Moon evolution that anything of an animal nature could arise. There had to be an influence from outside. We are not, in fact, told in Genesis of anything being active from without up to the end of the third day of creation. And the transition from the third to the fourth day is an important one in that we are told that on the fourth day light forces, beings of light, began to be active from outside. So just as in the Moon evolution the sun shone upon the moon from outside, now both the sun and the moon shine upon the earth from outside. What we are saying is no less than that up to this point all those forces could be active which were within the earth itself. Up to this moment in time everything could be recapitulated which represented earlier stages, and those things which were centralized in the earth itself could arise anew. Thus we saw yesterday that the spirit of the elohim brooding over the waters was a recapitulation of the condition of warmth; that at the moment designated by the words 'Let there be light' the entry of light was recapitulated; how at the point where the forces of the sound ether broke in and separated what became the upper realm from what became the lower realm the sound ether stage was recapitulated. This was presented in the description of the so-called second day of creation. Then we saw that life ether burst in on the so-called third day of creation, and out of the earth element, out of the new condition, there came forth all that can be brought about by the life ether—the realm of sprouting green. But for anything of an animal nature to find a place on our earth there had to be a repetition of forces working in from outside, light shining in from outside. Hence it is absolutely in accordance with the facts that there should be no mention in Genesis of anything of an animal nature until after we have been told of forces working upon the earth from cosmic space. Up to that time Genesis speaks only of the plant realm; all the beings included in the developing earth were at the plant stage. The animal species could only begin when the beings of the light influenced the earth from surrounding space.

What came about then is described in Genesis in words of which there are innumerable translations. The English authorised version is: 'And God said . . . let them be for signs, and for seasons and for days, and years.' We have now come across a few commentators who have begun to think. But it is the fate of commentators today, where people have utter scorn for getting down to the real fundamentals, that they carry out the beginning of thinking but cannot think through to the end. I have come across some commentators who have actually reached the point of acknowledging that the usual rendering is nonsense. I should like to meet the person who can actually make any sense of these words. What is really being said?

If we want to render these words faithfully and with a real sense of the associations they would have had for the ancient Hebrew sage, and put them into a thoroughly philological translation, we should have to say that once more it is not a matter of signs but of the activity of living beings making themselves known in the form of successive events in time. A correct translation would be: 'And the elohim appointed beings to regulate the course of time for the creatures on earth, to be the regulators of particularly impressive moments, of larger and smaller periods of time, which are usually rendered as "year" and "day".' Thus a reference is made to those beings who are one rank below the rank of the archai, and who regulate life. The tasks performed by the time spirits, the archai, lie a stage lower than the tasks of the elohim. Then come the regulators, the sign fixers for those things which have to be carried out within the archai's sphere of activity. These beings are none other than the archangels. Thus we may venture to say that, coinciding with Genesis telling us that not only is something taking place in the body of the earth itself but that forces are working into it from outside, Genesis also says that at that same moment those beings make their appearance who were connected already with the Sun existence, the regulating archangels who are one stage lower than the archai. While these archai themselves are still active as aeons, as it were, for the deployment of their forces they make use of the archangels, the light bearers, who act out of our earth's surroundings. In other words, the way the archangels work is that from out of cosmic space, by way of the constellations of the light beings surrounding the earth, they carry out the tremendous decrees which are actually laid down by the archai.

Those who were present at the lectures I gave in Christiania will remember that right up to today the archai are still there behind what we are accustomed to calling the spirit of the age.[5] If we look around at the way our world affairs are organized we shall find that at any given time there are a number of nations. You will be able to say of these national groups that for a specific period an all-encompassing time spirit rules, while side by side with this spirit, beings subordinate to him rule the several folk spirits. Just as today the spirits of the age are in control and behind them are the archai—I described this in my Christiania lectures—so behind the folk spirits are the archangels; in a certain way they *are* the folk spirits. Genesis actually points to the fact that even in times when man was actually not yet there, these spiritual beings were the organizing powers.

So we must say that it was the elohim who brought light into existence; they manifested themselves through the light. But for the lesser activities within the light they appointed the archai indicated by the word *yom*, and who rank next below them among the hierarchies, and beside them they placed the beings who must of necessity be woven into the web of existence, so that as well as the activity of the light there could also be the activity of darkness which goes with it. Beside *yom* they put *laila*, which is usually translated as 'night'. There then had to be further progress, further specialization in evolution and, for this, other beings had to be taken from the ranks of the hierarchies. So when we say that the elohim or spirits of form manifested themselves through the light and placed the affairs of light and darkness in the charge of the archai, we have to continue by saying that the elohim now took another step and, specializing further, appointed the archangels to the task of not only calling to life plant nature which is presented as an outer manifestation but of now calling forth inner life which is a reflection of outer existence; they entrusted to the archangels the activity which has to stream down upon our earth from outside, so that not only can the plant species burst forth but also the animal species with its inwardly active life of mental image and sensation can arise.

Thus we see, if we know how to interpret these things correctly, that Genesis points clearly to the archangels. If you think about what the usual run of commentators say, you will always feel dissatisfied. But if you turn for help to the same source from which Genesis arose, esoteric science, you will be able to throw light on whichever part you are looking at. It will all appear to you in a new light. And this ancient document which—because of the impossibility of translating the living words of old into our own language, would otherwise inevitably remain incomprehensible—will endure as a document which speaks to humankind for all time.

Elemental Existence and the Spiritual Beings Behind It. Jehovah-Elohim

During these lectures I shall try to throw light on the Genesis story of creation from all kinds of different aspects. As with all such presentations we must never lose sight, of course, of our anthroposophical principles of which the first and foremost is to enquire into the facts of spiritual life. So too, what is of primary importance as regards the Genesis story is to ascertain what were the supersensible events, the supersensible facts which preceded the visible course of earth's evolution. Only after that do we attach special importance to finding confirmed in ancient documents of various ages and peoples what we have first established independently of any documents, out of spiritual research itself. In fact it is our own endeavours which enable us to acquire the right feeling, the proper attitude of reverence for what sounds into our innermost souls from far-off times and peoples. This connection affords us the possibility of re-acquainting ourselves with those times which we ourselves will of course have lived in during other incarnations, and of re-forming links with what must have affected us in past epochs. This is how we have to understand the underlying purpose of this course of lectures.

We have endeavoured in the past few days to form an idea of how to rediscover in Genesis the spiritual beings we know from spiritual science. We have already partly succeeded in this. We have constantly borne in mind that the things which we meet with in the outer world, even what we meet with on the lower levels of clairvoyant consciousness—and in Genesis we are basically dealing all the time with facts of clairvoyant consciousness—are *maya*, illusion; that our usual view of the sense world, as we first of all know it, is *maya*, illusion. This is a statement which is familiar to anyone who has anything to do with spiritual science. In fact, anyone who has studied spiritual science for any length of time will not be ignorant of the fact that the lower regions of clairvoyance, everything to do with the etheric and astral world, also belong in a higher sense to this sphere of illusion. We do not reach the actual foundation of existence—as far as we can attain it—until we have penetrated beyond these regions to life's deeper sources. We must keep reminding ourselves of this; and we must not be content merely to voice this as a theory. The conviction must get right into our flesh and blood that in clinging to external existence we are surrendering to illusion. On the other hand to ignore outer existence, to prize it too lightly, is also one of the great illusions to which human beings can succumb.

Let us now have a look at something we have been talking a great deal about over the past few days, namely the realm of the elements, which is the next realm we can reach behind the physical realm, the one we perceive with our physical senses. Let us have a look at the realm of the elements described by spiritual science as existing behind manifestations of the nature of earth, water, air, fire or warmth, and the more ethereal manifestations of the nature of light, sound and life. Let us look at this elemental realm. We try to acquire ideas about the nature of these manifestations and to keep firm hold of these ideas. We achieve nothing if we assume an air of intellectual superiority, which can very easily become widespread among theosophical devotees, and simply say: 'That is all *maya*, of course!' For the real beings are revealing themselves through this *maya*. And if we refuse to pay any attention to the manifestations, if we spurn getting to know anything about the tools and instruments through which they reveal themselves, we have no means of making existence comprehensible. We must realize that when we say 'water', 'air', and so on, we are referring to expressions, to manifestations of real spirituality, but if we refuse to have anything to do with this *maya* we shall not have the least idea about what is there behind it. So it is essential for us to realize fully that the series of elements are expressions, manifestations, revelations of spiritual beings.

Let us have a look now, from the anthroposophical point of view, at the earthly element. We know well enough by now that there was no question of there being anything of the nature of an earthly element on ancient Saturn, nor on ancient Sun nor ancient Moon. We know that evolution had to wait until our planet came into existence before the earth element could be added to the warmth element of Saturn, the air element of Sun, and the water element of Moon. We know that each step in evolution can only proceed through the work of spiritual beings. If we want to place the physical body, the lowest member of our human existence, in the life of the elements, we may say that it has made its way from the first rudiments which it acquired on ancient Saturn, from the state of warmth, through the state of air on Sun, through the state of water on Moon, and progressed as far as the present earth state. Thus we have in our own external physical body something of which we can say that it has passed through an existence of weaving warmth, an existence as an airlike body, an existence as a watery body, and has progressed as far as an earthly existence. We know, too, who the beings were who took part in the work on ancient Saturn, fashioning the first evolutionary condition of the human physical body. Remember what I presented in *An Outline of Esoteric Science* and elsewhere, that to begin with certain spiritual beings worked on ancient Saturn who had passed through their lower stages of evolution in a long distant past, and who were already so far advanced that they were so to speak able to sacrifice their own coporeality to supply the foundation, the basic substance for ancient Saturn. In the order of the hierarchies these spiritual beings are none other than those whom we call the spirits of will. Into the substance thus provided, which had been offered as a sacrifice by the spirits of will, the other hierarchies then put their work. The spirits of personality worked their own way into it, developing their own humanity in this will substance. It was this very will substance which worked on ancient Saturn as the warmth element, and it was in this warmth that the first rudiments of the human physical body were formed.

But you must not imagine that beings such as the spirits of will might stop working at a certain stage. Even though they did the bulk of the work on Saturn they continued working during the evolutionary process on Sun, Moon and earth, and kept up a certain connection with the substance with which they first made their sacrifice. In fact we saw how during the ancient Sun evolution the element of warmth was transformed into the element of air, moving as it were in a downward direction towards densification. A process such as this, which appears to be a densification of warmth into air, is nevertheless only *maya*, giving us the illusion of densification. Within this process itself a spiritual activity is going on. And anyone wanting to get to the core of the matter has to ask which of the hierarchies brought the more rarefied warmth substance into the coarser condition of the substance of air. It was these very spirits of will who made their sacrifice in the substance of warmth! We can describe their activity by saying that during ancient Saturn evolution they were advanced enough to be able to pour out their own substance as warmth, to offer it as a sacrifice, so that their fire streamed into the planetary existence of ancient Saturn. Then during the ancient Sun existence they condensed this, their fire, into a gaseous element. It was also they who during the Moon evolution condensed their gaseous element to liquid, and during earth evolution they condensed liquid still further to the earth element, to solid matter. So when we look about us in the world today and see solid matter, we have to tell our-selves that there are the forces of beings at work in it without which it would be utterly impossible for solid matter to exist, forces belonging to beings whose very substance flowed forth as warmth into ancient Saturn; and they made this substance coarser and coarser until it reached the solid state which is now firmly held together by their powerful forces. And if we want to know who it is that brings this about, if we want to look beyond the *maya* of solid matter, we have to say that behind everything of a solid nature there is the active work of the spirits of will, the thrones. Thus even in our present earthly existence the spirits of will are still present. This throws a new light on what we are told in Genesis.

When we are told that what is expressed in Genesis as *bara* is a kind of meditative activity of the elohim, we have to say that the elohim re-created out of their meditation, as a kind of memory, something I have described as a complex of exis-tence. But in a certain way there happened to the elohim what happens to us when we create something out of memory, though we of course carry out this activity at a much lower level. Let us choose a comparison. Think of a human being going to sleep in the evening. Where his own subjective consciousness is concerned his world of thought and feeling sinks into oblivion as he passes into a condition of sleep. Suppose the last thought he had in the evening was, say, of a rose, a rose that was beside him when he fell asleep. This thought sinks into oblivion. In the morning the thought of the rose re-appears. If the rose were not still there the person would only have the thought. You must distinguish between these two facts. The one is the calling up in memory of the image of the rose, which could occur even if the rose had been removed. So you have the thought, the memory of the rose. But if the rose is still there you also perceive the visible rose. That is the other fact. I want you to distinguish in a similar manner these two things in what I have described as the cosmic meditation of the elohim. So when we are told that on the third 'day' of creation a cosmic meditation takes place and that the elohim divide the water from the land, that they separate out the solid element and call it earth, we must also include in the picture the cosmic meditation of the elohim, from whom this thought comes forth creatively. But in what appears in their meditations we have to see the spirits of will at work, bringing forth yet again real being, objectively, from out of themselves. This is how the spirits of will work, and this is how they have worked from the beginning in everything of an earth nature.

You must make yourselves familiar with such ideas. You must get used to the thought that in the things closest to us, and which we often regard as very lowly, we may meet very high and exalted beings. It is easy enough to say of the solid element that it is only 'matter'. And some people may be tempted to say that it is no concern of the spiritual investigator for, after all, matter is only of minor importance. Why bother with it? We rise above matter to a spiritual level. Anyone who thinks like this is ignoring the fact that through countless ages lofty spiritual beings have been working in the substance he wants to discredit, to bring it into this solid state. Actually, if our feeling life were to penetrate through the elemental covering of the earth to what has made this earth covering solid, it would be the natural thing to feel the deepest reverence and the greatest respect for the exalted beings we call the spirits of will, who have laboured so long in this earthly element to build the solid ground upon which we tread, and which we ourselves bear within us in the earthly constituents of our physical bodies. It is these spirits of will, whom in Christian esotericism we also call the thrones, who have in fact constructed—or rather condensed—the solid ground upon which we walk. The esotericists who gave names to what the spirits of will created within our earth existence called these spirits 'thrones', because they did indeed build 'thrones' which, all the time, are supporting us and giving us a firm foundation; and upon this all the other aspects of our earth existence will continue to be firmly and solidly 'enthroned'. These old expressions have an essential quality to which our feelings can respond with the greatest respect and admiration.

If we now go back up again from the solid to the watery element, we have to say that a longer time had to be spent on building up and densifying the earthly element than the watery, therefore we shall expect to find the fundamental forces behind the watery element belonging to beings of a lower hierarchy. For the condensation of this element into the condition it has around us today, it needed only the activity of the spirits of wisdom, kyriotetes or dominions, the next rank down in the hierarchies. Therefore whereas behind our solid foundations we see the spirits of will, behind what is not physical water but the forces which constitute the liquid element we have to see the activity of the spirits of wisdom or kyriotetes. If we go up to the airy element we have to see the next lowest hierarchy at work. In the activity of the air around us, to the extent that it is brought about by forces lying behind them, we have also to see the effect of the activity of certain spirits of the hierarchies. Just as the spirits of wisdom work in the watery element, the spirits of movement—the dynamis, mights, as we are accustomed to call them in Christian esotericism—are at work in the air. And when we ascend to the warmth element, the next stage of rarefaction, it is the spirits of the next hierarchy lower down, the spirits of form, exusiai, who are at work there, the spirits we have been speaking of for days as the elohim. Up to now we have been describing the spirits of form from quite a different side, namely as those who brooded in the warmth element. When we trace the order of the hierarchies from the spirits of will down through the spirits of wisdom and of movement we once again come to our elohim, to our spirits of form. You see how it all links up if you line them up properly.

If you now try to bring sensitive and perceptive feelings into all this, you will say that at the foundation of all we see around us with our senses there is an elemental realm. There is an element of earth, yet in reality there live within it the spirits of will; there is a fluid element in which in truth live the spirits of wisdom; an airy element within which in reality live the spirits of movement; and a warmth element wherein in truth live the spirits of form, the elohim.

However, we must not think that we can make a clear separation between these spheres; that we can draw rigid boundaries between them. The whole of earthly life is based on the fact that water, air and solid matter work into one another, and that warmth permeates everything. There is nothing of a solid nature that is not in a state of warmth. We find warmth everywhere within the other levels of elemental existence. Therefore we can also say that the activity of the elohim, the actual force behind the element of warmth, is to be found absolutely everywhere. It has poured itself out into everything. Although it required for its very existence the activity of the spirits of will, of wisdom and of movement, this element of warmth which is the manifestation of the spirits of form nevertheless interpenetrated all the other levels of existence during the earth stage. Therefore in the solid element we shall not only find the material basis of earth, the body of the spirits of will, but the body of the spirits of will permeated and interwoven by the elohim themselves, the spirits of form.

Let us now try to find in the sense realm the outer expression of what we have just stated. We have been describing things from the supersensible point of view, namely as an interweaving of the spirits of will, the thrones, and the spirits of form, the elohim. This is in the supersensible realm. But everything of a supersensible nature throws its shadow image into our world of sense. How does it display itself? That which is substantially the body, the essential being of the spirits of will, is the solid matter spread out around us. The commonly accepted idea of matter is an illusion. The ideas we have of matter are *maya*. When the seer turns his attention to the places where matter is supposed to lead its dubious existence, he does not find these fantastic ideas of physical matter, for those are an empty illusion. Matter as conceived by the physicist is pure fantasy. So long as these concepts are used merely as calculating devices, it is all right. But when people imagine they have discovered something real, they are dreaming. The theories of modern physics are in fact dreams. In so far as physicists take note of facts, and describe actual solid facts—for example giving descriptions of what the eye can see and what can be deduced from this by doing calculations—then they are on to true reality. But as soon as they begin to speculate about atoms, molecules and so on, as if these were simply material entities, then they begin to hallucinate on a grand scale; which reminds me of Felix Balde's ducats in my mystery play, when he says in the temple: 'Fancy telling someone from whom you want to buy something: "I won't pay for it with real coin, but I promise you I will condense some ducats out of mist!" '[1] This crude simile really does give a fair idea of the sort of theory of physics that readily accepts that whole universe can come forth from primordial mist if the need for a world view can be paid for with the coinage offered in this domain by science. It is pure fantasy to take the existence of atoms, as envisaged today, to be real. So long as atoms are looked upon merely as counters or shorthand notes for what the senses actually show, we keep our feet on the ground. If we want to penetrate behind the sense perceptible layer, however, we have to rise to the realm of the spirit, where we reach the living movement of a basic substance which is none other than the bodily nature of the thrones, permeated by the activity of the spirits of form. And how is this projected into our sense world? Around us we have an expanse of solid matter, which is at no stage amorphous, however. Formlessness only results from the fact that basically all existence, pushing as it does towards form, bursts apart or is crushed. None of the dust we find in the world is dust by normal tendency. It is the result of a wearing down process. Matter as such has the urge to take on form; everything solid tends to become crystalline. Thus we can say that what we call the substance of the thrones and of the elohim is impelled into our sense world, announcing itself as the solid matter all around us. Through the fact of it manifesting as what we call matter, it announces itself as the essential being of the thrones; in so far as this basic substance takes on shape and form, it announces itself as the outer revelation of the elohim.

Look with what spiritual insight names were given in ancient times! Seers of old realized: When we look at the material world it is proclaiming itself in the substance of the thrones, but it is permeated by a force which wants to give a form to everything. Hence the name 'spirits of form'! In all these names there is a hint of the reality they stand for. Just look at the urge to crystallization going on around us. You have, at a lower level, the elohim themselves, the spirits of form, revealing outwardly the drive they have to assume crystal form, and exercising this tremendous force and movement in the substance of the thrones. They are the smiths, forging in the warmth element the crystalline forms of the different earths and metals out of the formless substance of the spirits of will. They are the spirits who in their activity of warmth are at the same time the forming element of existence.

When we look at things this way we gaze into the active life stirring beneath the surface of our existence. And this accustoms us to see *maya* or illusion in everything that approaches us externally. But we must not come to a standstill over the mere theory that the external world is *maya*. That achieves nothing. The statement only makes sense if we penetrate through the separate aspects of *maya* and find in each instance the real being behind it. This is the way to accustom ourselves to see in everything that happens around us something which, though certainly illusion, has truth in it. Semblance is after all semblance. As such it is a fact, but we do not understand it if we stop at its semblance value. We are only justified in respecting and valuing it as semblance if we go on beyond its appearance.

In our modern abstract way of looking at things we muddle everything up. The seers of old did no such thing. It was not so straightforward for them that they saw the same superficial forces in everything, as the modern physicist does, who insists on embracing meteorology as well as physics within his sphere. For who today doubts that the same forces which are at work in elemental existence—in solid matter, fluids and so on—are active too within the atmosphere when clouds form, when water masses into cloud. I know quite well that the modern physicist cannot help assuming that, as a physicist, he can aspire to be a meteorologist too, and that for him things only make sense if he applies the same laws to the formation of the watery masses that surround our earth as clouds as he does to earthly existence. To the seer things are not as simple as that. As soon as things are traced back to their spiritual sources you cannot expect to see the same thing everywhere. Different forces are at work when a form of gas condenses to liquid directly on to the earth than are at work when gas or vapour forms watery cumuli. When contemplating the way water arises in the atmosphere around us, the seer cannot say that water comes into being there in exactly the same way as it does on the ground; that the water hovering above us comes into existence in the same way as water condenses in the soil or on the ground itself. For the truth is that the beings who play their part in cloud formation are different from those who are active in the formation of water. What I have just been saying regarding the participation of the hierarchies in our elemental existence applies only on the earth from its centre up to where we ourselves stand, but the same forces do not suffice to form the clouds as well. Other beings are at work there. The scientific theory derived from modern physics is based on a very simple hypothesis. First it discovers certain physical laws, and then it says that these laws apply to the whole of existence. It overlooks all the differences in the different spheres of existence. It acts on the principle that in the night all cows are grey; but things are not the same everywhere; they are very different in the different domains!

Anyone who has become aware through clairvoyant investigation that on our earth the thrones or the spirits of will govern the earth element, the spirits of wisdom the watery element, the spirits of movement the airiform element and the elohim the element of warmth, will gradually come to realize that in the gathering of the clouds, in that unique process going on in the circumference of our earth in which the watery vapour turns to water, beings belonging to the hierarchy of the cherubim are at work. When we look at the solid matter of our elemental existence we see the elohim co-operating with the thrones. When we look upward to the airy element, even though it is governed by the spirits of movement, we see the cherubim at work in it, so that the water rising up from the realm of the spirits of wisdom can accumulate as clouds. It is just as true that the cherubim govern the earth surroundings as it is true that the thrones, the spirits of wisdom and the spirits of movement govern the elemental existence on our earth. If we now look into the active essence of these cloud formations themselves, into their hidden depths, which are only revealed now and then, we are aware of lightning and thunder coming forth. This is not something which comes from nothing. The seer knows that the spirits whom we call the seraphim move and have their being in this activity. Remaining within the limits of our earth sphere, including the circumference of our earth, we have now found every one of the hierarchical ranks.

Thus in what we experience with our senses we see the manifestations of hierarchical activity. It would be utter nonsense to imagine that what you see when lighning flashes forth from the clouds is the same as what you see when you strike a match. Every time electricity, the element active in lightning, comes forth from matter, quite different forces are at work, namely the seraphim. So we can find the totality of the hierarchies in the earth's environment just as we can find them out there in the cosmos. For the hierarchies, as we see, also extend their activity to what is in our immediate environment.

When you go through the pages of Genesis and look at the mighty course of world evolution depicted there, you discover that all the previous stages taking place during the ancient Saturn, Sun and Moon existences are being repeated, and that man finally emerges as the crowning achievement of evolution. We have to realize that Genesis is telling us that the being and activity of all the hierarchies is engaged in what is occurring there, and that it is all being concentrated, as it were, on the final product of earth evolution, that supersensible being—for initially it was supersensible—of whom it is said that the elohim resolved to create it, saying: 'Let us make man.' They wove together all their separate talents into one communal activity. All the abilities which they brought with them from earlier stages were woven together so as finally to create man. Indeed, all the hierarchies who preceded man, and whom we call seraphim, cherubim, thrones, spirits of wisdom, spirits of movement and spirits of form, archai or spirits of personality, fire spirits or archangels and angels—we have found all of them, they all moved and had their being in all that existed. And if we follow the Genesis account up to the crowning of the structure on the sixth 'day' of creation with the appearance of man, if we review the whole life and essence of pre-human earthly evolution, we find that all the various hierarchies are already there. All of these hierarchies had to join forces to prepare what finally appeared as man.

Thus we may venture to say that the seer or seers among whom Genesis arose were aware that all the hierarchies we have named had to contribute to the preparatory stage of man. But they also had to be aware that for the creation of man himself, for the final crowning of this whole sequence of the hierarchies, help had to come from another direction, one that is still higher in a certain respect than any of these hierarchies. So we turn our gaze beyond the seraphim to an as yet unknown and only dimly sensed divine being. Let us try for a moment to follow up the activity of one of the members of the hierarchical order, the elohim let us say. Before they had reached the decision to crown their works by creating man it sufficed for them to work in harmony with the activity of the other hierarchies up to the seraphim. But then help had to come from the direction to which, out of a dim presentiment, we have to lift our spiritual gaze; it had to come from a realm above that of the seraphim. For the elohim to raise their creative activity to these dizzy heights, to obtain help from this source, something had to occur the significance of which we want to try to understand. They had, so to speak, to grow beyond themselves. They had to acquire a greater ability than was theirs during the preparatory stages of the work. To crown their work completely and carry it through to the finish the elohim had to unfold still higher powers. The elohim as a group had to grow beyond themselves. Let us try to form an idea of how such a thing can happen, and do this by making use of a rather humble illustration. Take the development of a human being.

When we see a tiny child on the threshold of earthly existence we know that he has not yet developed what we call an integrated consciousness. It is only after some time that he even calls himself 'I', which brings unity into the consciousness. It is only then that the contents of his soul life become knit together in an integrated consciousness. The child grows to a further stage through the drawing together of the various activities which in the baby are still decentralized. Thus in the human being this drawing together signifies an advance to a higher stage. We can think of the progressive development of the elohim as analogous to this. During the preparatory stages of human creation they learnt a certain activity. Whilst performing this activity they themselves learnt something and contributed something towards raising themselves to a higher stage. As a group they have now attained to a kind of unified consciousness; they have not remained simply a group but have become a unity. This unity became a kind of being. This fact is an extremely important one. Up to now I was only able to tell you that the various elohim each had his own special capacity. Each of them was able to contribute something to the common resolve, the common image of the human being they wanted to form; and yet this was still only an idea upon which they could co-operate. To begin with it was not real. Something real existed only after they had created the common product. But in the course of this work itself they developed to a higher stage, they made their unity a reality, so that they were no longer seven but a sevenfold whole. We can now speak of an 'elohimhood' which reveals itself in a sevenfold way. This 'elohimhood' only arose in course of time. The elohim raised themselves to this level.

The Bible knows this. The Bible recognizes the idea that the elohim were previously members of a group and then formed themselves into a unity. That first they co-operated as members of a group and were later on governed by a common organism. And this real unity of elohim in which the single elohim are active as organs of a body, is called in the Bible Jehovah-Elohim.[2] This gives us a more profound idea of Jehovah than was possible before. This is why the Bible at first speaks simply of the elohim and then, when the elohim themselves have progressed to a higher stage, to a unity, it starts speaking of Jehovah-Elohim. This the deeper reason why, at the end of the book of creation, the name of Jehovah suddenly appears. This shows how necessary it is to have recourse to occult sources if one wants to understand such things.

What does Bible criticism of the nineteenth century make of this? It says: We find in one passage the name elohim and in another the name Jehovah. Clearly the two passages derive from two different religious traditions, and we have to distinguish between what has come from a people who worshipped the elohim and what has come from a people who worshipped Jehovah. And the person who wrote the account of creation used both names indiscriminately, and we have to separate them again! This line of research has gone so far that today we have so-called 'rainbow Bibles', with what is said to derive from the one source printed in blue and what comes from the other printed in red. There *are* such Bibles! Only, unfortunately, sometimes the antecedent is blue and the final clause red, because the first part of the sentence is said to derive from one people and the rest of it from the other. It is astonishing that the main and subordiante clauses should fit so beautifully together that any old collator could combine them!

Bible commentators have gone to great pains over this, perhaps more so than over any other scientific or historical research, but it only fills us with sadness, and a deep sense of tragedy. An account which is meant to tell us about the most profound spiritual matters has lost its connection with its spiritual source and origin. It is as though someone were to say 'We find quite a different style in the second part of *Faust* if we compare the passage containing the words of Ariel with the doggerel in Part I. It is impossible that one and the same person could have written them both, therefore Goethe must be a mythical figure.' Through being cut off from occult sources the fruit of this immense and devoted labour is worth as much as the conclusion of someone who denies the existence of Goethe because he cannot believe that two such different things as the style of *Faust Part I* and *Faust Part II* could have been written by the same person. This gives us a glimpse into a deep tragedy of human life, one that stresses the necessity that minds should again turn to the sources of spiritual life. Spiritual knowledge will only be possible if people set out once more in search of the living spirit. They *will* do so, for to do so is an irresistible urge of the human soul. And all the strength with which anthroposophy can inspire us comes from our confidence that there is this urge in the human soul activating our hearts to seek once again for a connection with spiritual sources, and which will bring us to understand the true basis of religious documents. Let us fill ourselves with this confidence, and then we shall reap the genuine fruits of a theme which should lead us to the living spirit.

Lecture 7, 23 August 1910

The Structure of the First and Second 'Days' of Creation. The Work of Elemental Beings on Human Organs

In our efforts to understand existence it is our practice to trace the course of some aspect of its development, and we have had many opportunities of becoming familiar with the idea that everything we perceive around us is in course of evolution. We must get used to applying the idea of evolution on a larger scale in spheres not usually associated with it today—for instance, people hardly think of real evolution with regard to the life of the soul. We probably do recognize it as it manifests outwardly in the life of the individual between birth and death. But so far as humanity as a whole is concerned people immediately think of evolution as an upward ascent from lower animal forms, and draw the conclusion—a somewhat fanciful one even from the standpoint of what can be known today—that higher organisms can develop from lower ones, the human organism can evolve from animal organisms in an absolutely straightforward way, with no further input. It is of course not my task in these lectures to show in detail, as I have often done, that our present consciousness has undergone a large-scale evolution, that the kind of consciousness, the kind of soul life we have today, was preceded by another form of consciousness. We have often described this earlier form as a kind of lower clairvoyant consciousness. With our modern consciousness external perception provides us with mental images of external objects. But that other, earlier form of consciousness can best be studied if we look back to the ancient Moon evolution.

The most outstanding difference between the evolution of ancient Moon and that of our present earth is that the ancient type of clairvoyance, a kind of picture consciousness, has been superseded by the present-day consciousness of objects. For many years I have been calling attention to this, and years ago you were able to read the information I gave from the akashic record on the subject of evolution. It appeared in the early essays of the magazine *Lucifer Gnosis*.[1] There, I pointed out that the old dreamlike picture consciousness which we had in former times has developed into our earthly consciousness, into what today gives us consciousness of external things, of what we call external things in space in contrast to what we ourselves are in our inner being. This ability to distinguish between external objects and our own inner life is what characterizes our present state of consciousness. When we have an object in front of us, this rose for instance, we say: 'This rose is in space. It is separate from us. We are in different places.' We perceive the rose and make a mental image of it. The mental image is inside us and the rose is outside. Being able to distinguish between outer things and inner things is the mark of our present-day consciousness. Consciousness on ancient Moon was not like that. Beings with an ancient Moon consciousness made no such distinction. Suppose that when you looked at the rose you were not aware that the rose was outside and that you were making a mental image of it, but that you had an awareness of the rose hovering in space and of its actual essence not being confined to the space it occupied but spreading outward into space and actually being within you too. In fact we could go further. Suppose that when you looked at the sun you were not conscious that the sun was up there and you were down here but that you were aware that while you were forming a mental image of the sun the sun was within you, that you were taking hold of the sun in a more or less spiritual way. Then there would be no distinction between inside and outside. If you can grasp this, then you will have arrived at a real under-standing of one of the characteristic qualities of the kind of consciousness which belonged to ancient Moon.

Another characteristic of this consciousness was that it was pictorial, so that things did not appear directly as objects but as symbols, just as dreams often make use of symbols today. For instance in a dream a fire external to ourselves appears as the symbol or image of a radiant being. Things were perceived in a similar way by the ancient Moon consciousness, inwardly but also pictorially. It was a pictorial consciousness per-meated with the quality of inwardness. And there was yet another essential difference between that consciousness and the one we have today. It did not have the effect at all as though external objects were there. For the ancient Moon consciousness what we today call our environment, what we perceive as sense objects belonging to the plant, mineral and human realm, were not there at all. What was there was somewhat similar, though on a lower, dreamlike level, to what is experienced in the soul today when the power of seership, clairvoyant consciousness, arises. The first awakening of clairvoyant consciousness is of such a nature that at first it does not extend to external beings. This is a source of countless deceptions for those who by means of esoteric development, for instance, are developing the gift of clair-voyant faculties.

Such a training progresses by stages, of course. There is a first stage of clairvoyance in which a person develops certain things and sees certain things in his environment. But he would be making a mistake if he were straightway to think that what he perceives in his environment, let us say in spirit space, is actually spiritual reality. In my mystery play, Johannes

Thomasius is going through this stage of astral clairvoyance.[2] Let me remind you of the scenes which rise up before his soul as he sits in meditation down-stage, and feels the spiritual world dawning in his soul. Pictures arise, and the first of these is the spirit of the elements showing him pictures of people he already knows in life. In the play, Johannes Thomasius has made the acquaintance of Professor Capesius and Dr Strader. He knows them from the physical plane, and has formed certain impressions of them there. When, after going through great pain, his clairvoyant capacity breaks through, he sees them again; in fact he sees them in strange forms. He sees Capesius as a young man, as he was at the age of twenty-five or twenty-six, and not as he is at the moment when he, Johannes Thomasius, sits meditating; and he does not see Dr Strader in the present, either, but as he is bound to look when he has become an old man in the present incarnation. These and many other pictures pass through Johannes Thomasius' soul. One can only present this dramatically if the pictures which come alive in the soul in meditation actually appear on the stage. It would be a mistake for Johannes Thomasius to regard this as deception. That would be quite wrong. The only right attitude to all this would be to realize that he cannot yet know to what extent this is deception or reality. He does not know whether what the pictures are showing him is an external spiritual reality or not; that is, he does not know whether it is something inscribed in the akashic record or whether he has expanded his own self to make a world. It could be both of these, and he must recognize that fact. What he lacks is the gift to distinguish between spiritual reality and picture consciousness. He has to admit that. And it is not until the moment when devachanic consciousness sets in, when in devachan he perceives the spiritual reality of a person whom he knows on the physical plane—Maria—that he is able to look back and to discriminate between reality and what is simply picture consciousness. Thus you can see that in the course of his esoteric development a human being has to pass through a stage in which he is surrounded by pictures but is quite unable to distinguish between manifestations of spiritual reality and the pictures themselves. The scenes of the mystery play reveal, of course, real spiritual realities. For instance, the way Professor Capesius appears is a true picture of the young Capesius, as inscribed in the akashic record, and the way Dr Strader appears is the real Strader as he will be in old age. In the play they are meant to be real, only Johannes Thomasius does not know that the figures he sees are real.

The stage of consciousness I have described was experienced on ancient Moon, only at a lower, more dreamlike level, so that no faculty of discrimination was possible. The ability to discriminate only began later, and you must thoroughly familiarize yourselves with what I have just said. Let us hang on to the fact that the clairvoyant lives his way into a kind of picture consciousness. But during the ancient Moon evolution the pictures which arose were in the main quite different from the objects of our earthly consciousness; and the same thing applies today in the early stages of clairvoyance. The clairvoyant does not at first see external spiritual beings at all; he sees pictures, and the question is: What do these pictures signify? You know, in the first stages of clairvoyance they are not expressions of real external spiritual beings at all but, if I may say so, a kind of organ consciousness. This is a pictorial presentation, a projection in space, of what is actually going on inside ourselves. And as the clairvoyant begins to develop these forces in himself, he can, to give an actual example, have the feeling he is perceiving two luminous globes far away in space. Two pictures, that is, of globes shining brightly in certain colours. If he were then to think to himself: 'Somewhere outside me there are two beings', the probability is that he would be quite wrong; at any rate that would be the case to begin with. For the fact is that his clairvoyance is projecting outward into space forces which are at work in himself, and seeing them as two globes. These two globes could represent what is at work in his astral body, bringing about in him the power of sight in his two eyes. This power of sight can be projected outwards in the form of two globes. In actual fact it is inner forces which are presenting themselves as external phenomena in astral space, and it would be the greatest mistake for something like this to be taken to herald the external presence of spiritual beings.

It would be a still greater error if, right from the beginning, with the help of a little bit of questionable assistance, one were to hear voices, and immediately interpret them as inspiration from outside. This is the greatest error to which one can fall prey. It will hardly be anything else but an echo of an inner process; and while what appears in images of colour and form usually represents fairly sound inner processes, voices are as a rule signs of pretty chaotic things going on in the soul. The best thing for anyone to do who begins hearing voices is to cultivate the greatest mistrust in what they say. So you see that the beginning of pictorial imagery must under all circum-stances be undertaken with the greatest care. It is a kind of organ consciousness, a projection of one's own inner being into space. During the ancient Moon evolution it was normal that the consciousness possessed then was a consciousness of the organs. At the Moon stage human beings scarcely per-ceived anything beyond what was happening within them at the time.

I have often recalled an important saying of Goethe: 'The eye was formed by the light for the light.'[3] This saying should be taken extremely seriously. All the organs we human beings have were formed by our environment. And philosophy is being very superficial if it only stresses one half of the truth, namely that without eyes human beings could not perceive light. For the other important half of the truth is that without light eyes could never have developed, and similarly without sound there would have been no ears. Looked at from a deeper point of view Kantianism is altogether superficial, because it only presents half the truth. The light weaving and flooding through cosmic space is the cause of the organs of sight. During the ancient Moon evolution the main task of the beings who took part in the upbuilding of our universe was the construction of our organs. First these organs have to be constructed, and then they are able to perceive. Our present objective consciousness is due to the fact that first of all the organs were constructed. The sense organs, as purely physical organs, were constructed as early as ancient Saturn, with the eye somewhat like the photographer's camera obscura. Purely physical apparatuses such as these can perceive nothing. They are constructed according to purely physical laws. During the ancient Moon evolution these organs were internalized. With regard to the eye we have to say that on ancient Saturn it was constructed to the extent that it was at most just a physical apparatus. At the Moon stage, through the sunlight shining in from outside, it was transformed into an organ of perception, an organ of consciousness. The essential thing about this activity during the ancient Moon evolution is that our organs were so to say drawn forth. During earth evolution the important thing is that light, for instance, influences the plants from outside and maintains their development. We see in the flora around us the product of this activity of the light. During the ancient Moon evolution light did not act in this way; it drew forth our organs, and what human beings perceived at that time was this work on their own organs. It was a per-ceiving of pictures, though these pictures appeared to be spread out in cosmic space. They were in fact nothing else than the expressions of the activity being carried out by the elements upon human organs. What the human being perceived during the ancient Moon evolution was his own construction, developing, as it were, out of his own being. He perceived his seeing eyes, the work being done in the course of his own inner becoming. Thus the outer world was an inner world, because the entire outer world was working on his inner being. And he made no distinction between what was outside and what was inside. He did not perceive the sun as an external object. He did not separate the sun from himself, but felt within himself his eyes coming into existence. And this active growth of his eyes expanded for him into a pictorial perception which filled space. This was how he perceived the sun, but it was an inner process. The characteristic thing about Moon consciousness was that the human being perceived a world of pictures around him, but these pictures represented inner growth, an inner building up of soul life. On Moon, then, the human being was enveloped in astral existence, and felt his own development to be an outer world. Nowadays it would be pathological to perceive this inner development as an outer world, so that one could not distinguish these pictures of the world outside which one is perceiving only as a reflection of one's own growth. But during the ancient Moon evolution it was the normal state of affairs. Human beings perceived within their own being the activity of those beings who later became the elohim. They perceived their activity somewhat as today you might perceive your blood flowing within you. It was within him, but it was reflected in pictures coming from outside.

But on ancient Moon such a consciousness was altogether the only one possible. For what happens on our earth has to happen in harmony with the whole cosmos. A consciousness such as human beings have on earth—with this distinction between what is outside and inside, with the perception of real objects being there outside us, as well as the perception of our also having an inner being—called for the whole evolutionary transition from Moon to earth, and quite a different form of separation occurred in our cosmic system. The kind of separation such as we have today between moon and earth was not there at all during the ancient Moon evolution. We have to think of what we call ancient Moon as though today's moon were still united with the earth. So all the other planets, including the sun, were quite differently constituted, and under the conditions of those times only a picture consciousness of that kind was possible. It was only after our whole cosmos had assumed the form it has as our earth environment that our present objective consciousness could develop.

So we must say that a consciousness such as human beings have on earth today was reserved for them until earth evolution. Not only did human beings not have it but nor did any of the other beings whom we speak of as belonging to one hierarchy or another. It would be foolish to think that because the angels passed through their human stage on ancient Moon they must therefore have had the kind of consciousness there that humankind has today on earth. This was not so, and this distinguishes them from human beings in that they went through their human stage with another consciousness. There is never a direct repetition of past circumstances. Each evolutionary impulse happens once only, and it happens for its own sake and not for the sake of repeating something. Therefore, to produce what we know today as earthly human consciousness, all the processes which have actually brought this earth about were needed and also the human being as he is today. It was impossible for such a form of consciousness to develop at an earlier stage of evolution. When we confront an object it is outside us and appears to us as an entity external to us. All previous kinds of consciousness, belonging to any of the beings we can name, made no distinction between what is outside and what is inside, so that it would have been nonsense for any of them to say: 'Something is appearing in front of me.' Even the elohim could not say that, for they had no such experience. They could only say: 'We move and have our being in the cosmos. We create, and in creating are aware of this our creation. There are no objects in front of us, no objects appear before us.' To say 'objects appear in front of us' conveys a situation in which we are confronted by something real formed in an external space from which we ourselves are separated. This did not come about even for the elohim until earth evolution. During the Moon evolution, when these elohim felt themselves weaving and working in the light which streamed from the sun upon Moon, they might have said to themselves: 'We feel our existence in this light; we feel ourselves descending, along with this light, into the beings who on ancient Moon are at the human level; we speed through space with this light.' But they could never have said: 'We see this light outside ourselves.' There was nothing like that during the Moon evolution. That was a totally new occurrence belonging to the earth.

When at a certain stage of evolution in Genesis the momentous words occur: 'And God said, Let there be light,' a new occurrence has to come about: that the elohim will not continue only to feel themselves flowing with the light but that the light is raying back to them from objects that appear to them from outside. This is expressed by the writer of Genesis when to the words 'And God said, Let there be light' he adds 'And God saw the light.' In this ancient document nothing is superfluous, nothing is meaningless. We could wish that among many other things people could learn from this document to write down nothing that is not pregnant with meaning, nothing that is merely empty words! The writer of Genesis wrote nothing that was unnecessary, nothing by way of commonplace embellishment to enhance the beauty of the creation of light; he does not make the elohim say anything like: 'We see the light and are pleased with ourselves that we have done it well.' The point of this brief statement is that something new has come about.

And it says even more than this. It does not only say 'And God saw the light' but that he saw that it was beautiful—or good.* I realize that in the Hebrew tongue there was not the distinction between 'beautiful' and 'good' that there is today. The Hebrew language has the same word for good as for beautiful. What is actually meant when people call something 'beautiful' or 'good'? In ancient Sanskrit, even in German, there is still an echo of what is meant. The word 'beautiful' covers all words in all languages which mean that an inner spiritual element appears in an external image. To be beautiful means that an inner quality appears outwardly. And the best concept we can connect with the word 'beauty' today is to hold fast to the idea that in the beautiful object an inner spiritual reality is being presented in a physical image on the surface, so to speak. We call something beautiful when we, as it were, see the spiritual element appearing in sense perceptible form. When does a marble statue become a thing of beauty? When through its outer form it produces the illusion that living spirit is in it. Beauty is the appearance of spirit in external form.

So when in Genesis we come to the words: 'God saw the light,' we can say that they convey the specific quality of earth evolution; but also that what could formerly only be experienced subjectively now appears externally; that the spirit presents itself in its outer manifestation. So the words which are usually translated as 'And God saw the light, and he saw that it was good,' can be paraphrased as: 'And the elohim experienced the consciousness that the element in which they previously existed now confronted them externally, and in

---

* The English authorized version uses the word 'good'.

this external phenomenon they experienced that the spirit was in the background expressing itself in the outer object'—for this is what the word 'beautiful' (or 'good') means. Wordy explanations will not help us to understand Genesis. What *will* help will be to keep our eyes open all the time for the secrets which are actually concealed in the words themselves. Then research will yield rich fruits; whereas all too many interpretations are nothing but tiresome pedantry.

But let us go a bit further. We saw that the characteristic features of Moon evolution could only arise because the sun separated from the Moon, and we appreciated the fact that during earth evolution the sun had also to separate from the earth, that a duality is essential for the existence of conscious being. The earth element had to withdraw. But a withdrawal of this kind involves something else, namely that the elemental conditions change with regard to both the moon and the sun. If you make a study of our present sun, even from a purely physical aspect, you are obliged to say that the conditions which we have on earth and which we call solid and liquid are not to be found on the physical sun. The most you can say is that the sun descends as far as the gaseous state. This is recognized even by modern physics. Such a splitting up of elemental conditions comes about through the separation of what was previously a unity.

We saw that the earth element develops in such a way that a kind of downward densification takes place from warmth right down to solid matter, and that the upper elements—light ether, sound ether, life ether—seem to press inwards from outside. However, we must not assume that a similar pattern occurs on the departing sun element. We had better have another look at the seven conditions of elemental existence. The first of these, the most rarefied state, is the one which contains and brings about life. Then comes what we can call number or sound ether, then light ether, and then warmth ether, and then we have air or gas, then water, and finally earth or solid matter. In the earth realm we shall find mainly the elements up as far as warmth. Warmth permeates our earth, whereas the earth only shares in the light in so far as the beings in its environment—or if you like the bodies in its environment—take part in the life of the earth. Light streams from the sun into the earth. If we want to locate the three higher elemental states—light ether, sound ether and life ether—we shall find them more in the region of the sun. It is in the earth sphere that we shall find the solid, fluid and gaseous elements, whereas warmth is spread over both the earth and the sun spheres. Light, spiritual sound and life should be allotted more to the sun. The forces that produce life belong more to the sun.

The first time this sun realm became separated was during the ancient Moon evolution. It was then that the light was for the first time active from without, but not then *as* light. I have just told you that the statement in Genesis 'And God saw the light' could not possibly have been spoken with regard to the Moon evolution. Then, one would have had to say that the elohim speeded through space with the light, were within the light, but saw it not. Just as today someone swimming in water moves forward in it without seeing it, at that time light was invisible, for it was a carrier of activity in cosmic space. It was with the coming of earth evolution that light began *to appear*, to be reflected by objects.

It was a natural further development that the situation regarding light during the Moon evolution should apply with regard to a somewhat higher condition during the earth evolution. We must expect that what applied to light on ancient Moon should, during earth evolution, apply to the sound ether. In other words, the same thing happens with sound ether during earth evolution that happened during the Moon evolution with light ether. This would imply that the elohim do not perceive the reflection of what we call spiritual sound in the same way as they do with light. Therefore if Genesis wanted to convey that evolution was advancing from light ether being active to sound ether being active, it would have to say something like: 'And the elohim saw the light in the developing earth, and saw that it was beautiful.' But it could not continue in the same vein and say: 'And during this phase the elohim perceived the sound ether,' but would have to say: 'They moved and had their being in it.' Nor could it be said of the second 'day' of creation that the elohim perceived the agitated movement separating the elements above from those below; this activity of the elohim could not be described as something they *perceived.* The words 'perceive' and 'beautiful' had to be omitted in Genesis, then the description would correspond with what can be observed through spiritual science. That is, the seer who wrote the Genesis account had, when describing the second 'day', to omit the words 'And God saw...'

Now look at Genesis. On the first 'day' it says: 'And God saw the light, that it was good.' On the second 'day' of creation you find in the most usual translations that it says, after the first 'day' has ended: 'And God said, Let there be a firmament in the midst of the waters, and let it divide the waters from the waters ... and it was so. And God called the firmament heaven. And the evening and the morning were the second day.' And the statement 'And God saw...' which is said of the first day, is omitted on the second day. Genesis describes the facts as we should expect them to be, from what we have been able to observe through the spiritual scientific method.

Here again is a knotty problem that the nineteenth-century commentators have not known what to make of. Some of them have said: What of it, if the words are omitted the second time? The writer must have forgotten to put them in. People should learn from Genesis that it not only records nothing irrelevant but also that it omits nothing that is relevant. The writer has not forgotten anything. There is the deepest reason why these words are not there for the second day of creation. Here we have another example—and I could quote a great many—of the kind of thing that fills us with immense appreciation and respect for a document like Genesis. We could learn a great deal from these ancient writers, who really did not need to pledge an oath, for once they recognized the truth they followed of their own accord the principle of telling the whole truth and nothing but the truth. They felt through and through that every word that stands there must be sacred to us, and equally that nothing essential must be omitted.

We have now gained an insight, a spiritual insight so to speak, into the composition of what are called the first and second 'days' of creation. Anyone who discovers through spiritual investigation what is behind these things might well say to himself on turning to his Bible: 'How wonderful it would be, overwhelmingly wonderful, if these subtle details, which can be discovered by conscientious spiritual investigation, should be corroborated by the words of the ancient seer who took part in the making of Genesis.' And when he finds that this overwhelming hope is verified, a wonderful feeling comes over him, the kind of feeling which should indeed fill our inner soul if we are once more to appreciate the sacredness of this ancient document, Genesis.

Stages of Human Development up to the Sixth 'Day' of Creation

In the course of these lectures we have formed a picture of the way the preparatory stages from the time of ancient Saturn, Sun and Moon contributed to our developing earth. We must of course always bear in mind that the focal point of our whole interest in the arising of the earth is the coming into being of man himself. We do know that the human being is, so to say, the first-born of our whole planetary evolution. When we turn our gaze back to ancient Saturn we are struck by the fact that in this condition of weaving warmth we can speak only of the first rudiments of physical man, and that as yet nothing existed of what surrounds us today in the animal, vegetable and mineral kingdoms. These kingdoms were added after the human kingdom was already there. Therefore we have to ask ourselves how the story of earth's creation according to Genesis is to be reconciled with the details of human evolution.

There is no doubt about it that in the course of these lectures we shall find full verification of what we are endeavouring to reach today by the spiritual scientific method. From a superficial reading of Genesis it might seem as though on the sixth 'day' of creation humankind suddenly appeared from nowhere, like a bolt from the blue. Yet we do know that the human kingdom is the all-important one, and that the other kingdoms are, as it were, by-products of the ascent to becoming man. So we should be interested in the question as to what was happening with regard to man on the 'days' preceding the sixth 'day'. Where is the human being to be found? If the coming into being of the earth presents a recapitulation of Saturn, Sun and Moon, we can presuppose that the coming into being of man is bound to show constant repetitions, and that we do not expect to find humankind only on the sixth 'day' of creation but before that. How is the apparent contradiction resolved, of Genesis not mentioning man previously?

First, there is something we have to notice, namely that when Genesis begins to speak of the creation of man it uses the word 'Adam',★ and in the priestly language of the ancient Hebrews the word 'Adam' corresponds more or less to our word 'man'. But we must understand more exactly what the word 'Adam' is expressing. The word called forth in the soul of a Hebrew sage an image which can perhaps be rendered as 'the earthly one'. Thus man is pre-eminently the *earth* being, the crowning of all *earth* existence, the final fruit of earth becoming. But everything which finally comes to maturity in the fruit is already inherent in the nature of the plant. We shall not discover man in the earlier 'days' of creation unless we realize that in reality it is not physical man that precedes the soul/spiritual man, but vice versa. We have to think of the physical, earthly man of today much in the same way as we think of a small quantity of water which we cool down and allow to solidify into ice. We have to think of soul/spiritual man as solidifying, condensing to earthly man through the work of the elohim on the sixth 'day', in the same way as water freezes to ice. The attaining of the sixth 'day' consisted in a condensation of the soul/spiritual part into solid earth man. On the preceding 'days' we must not expect to find man in the

---

★ In the English Authorised Version the word 'Adam' does not appear until ch.II, v.19—but in Hebrew the same word is used for 'man' (as in ch.I, v.26 onwards).

realm of what is forming supersensibly in the way of physical by-products or the laws of the physical by-products along the path to becoming human, but we shall find him, on the 'days' prior to the sixth, in a soul/spiritual condition. So when, in the words of Genesis, we say that on the first 'day' there were the inner mobile energy and the things that were manifesting outwardly we should not expect to find man in the earth realm on that first 'day' but as a soul/spiritual being in the periphery of the earth. We should say that this soul/spiritual being was the preparatory stage of man's earthly existence.

Today I want to correlate some of the findings of spiritual science with the Genesis account. When Genesis tells us that through cosmic thinking the two complexes of inner mobile energy and outward manifestation arise, what is it that is being prepared in the very first rudiments of the human being? When the spirit of the elohim weaves and broods through these complexes, which part of man is in course of preparation? It is what in our present-day spiritual scientific terminology we call the sentient soul; something we regard as belonging to our inner being today was being prepared, according to Genesis, on the first 'day' of creation up to the moment when it says: 'Let there be light; And there was light.' The sentient soul, as the soul/spiritual being of man, was present in all that was contained in the spiritual circumference. To put it more exactly, let us say that in the environment of the earth the first thing we shall look for is the sentient soul and place it at the time usually called the first 'day' of creation. Thus in the circumference of the earth, where the elohim and their ministering servants are carrying out their work on a soul/spiritual level, we have to see man's soul/spiritual being in this soul/spiritual atmosphere in a somewhat similar way to seeing clouds today in the airy atmosphere, and this is first of all the human sentient soul. Then human evolution advances, and if we watch what happens to the human being himself we can expect to find what we call the intellectual or perceptive soul. The sentient soul advances to the intellectual or perceptive soul, and in the circumference of the earth we have, on the second 'day' of creation, this kind of rarefaction of the sentient soul into the intellectual or perceptive soul. When the sound ether strikes into earth development, when the upper masses separate from the lower, there is, belonging to the upper sphere and weaving and moving therein, the human being who still only possesses the rudiments of the sentient soul and the intellectual or perceptive soul. Then, as the third step, we have to think of man as advancing to the stage of the consciousness soul. So we might think of the whole process which is presented in Genesis as the third 'day', as the scene in which down below on the earth under the influence of life ether, verdant life is springing forth according to species. The earth brings forth the basis of plant life—of course only supersensibly perceptible—and up above in the ether there weaves what we call the consciousness soul together with the sentient and the intellectual or perceptive soul.

Thus the soul/spiritual human being hovers in the periphery of the arising earth. It is as though man is within the substance of the various spiritual beings. So far he has no independent existence. It is as though he were being fashioned as an organ within the elohim, the archai and so on—as though he were a part of their bodies. Therefore it is natural that we are being told about these beings, for at this stage of the earth's becoming they alone are actual individualities, and to describe their destiny is to describe the destiny of the rudimentary human being as well. But you can imagine that, if humankind is one day to populate the earth, something like a gradual densification of the human being has to come about. This soul/spiritual form must gradually be clothed as it were in a body. At the end of what is called in the

Bible the third 'day' of creation we have the rudiments of a soul/spiritual human being, consisting of what we would today call the consciousness soul, intellectual or perceptive soul and sentient soul, and these have to be provided with an outer garment. The first thing that has to happen is that in these soul/spiritual spheres the human being has to acquire the garment of an astral body.

Let us try to imagine what we actually mean when we say that after the third 'day' of creation the human being must clothe himself in an astral body. Where today can we study the laws of the astral body as something separate from the physical body? Our astral bodies are a separate part of us when we are asleep, although the form they now have is quite different from what it was at the time of which Genesis speaks. We leave our etheric and physical bodies behind in bed, and we ourselves are then in our astral body which contains our ego.

Remember the many things I have told you over the years about the particular life of the astral body during sleep. From my *Outline of Esoteric Science* you will remember that when the astral body is outside the physical and etheric bodies currents go out from it and it begins to make connections with its cosmic surroundings. When in the morning you return from the sleeping to the waking state you have drawn strengthening forces from the whole cosmos. During the night your astral body became, by way of these connecting currents, part of the whole surrounding cosmos. It formed a connection with all the beings belonging to our earth. It sent its currents to Mercury, Mars, Jupiter and so on, and these planetary beings possess strengthening forces which give to the astral body what we need to enable us to continue our waking life on our return to our physical and etheric bodies. During the night our astral body streams forth and then becomes expanded to cosmic proportions. Clairvoyant consciousness sees the astral body passing out of the physical body when the person falls asleep. But in point of fact this is an inexact expression. The astral body winds its way out of the physical body in a spiral and moves as a cloud in spiral form. But this spectacle shows us only the beginning of the currents which emanate from the astral body. They really go right out into the spaces of the cosmos and gather and drink in the forces of the planets. If anyone wants to tell you that what an untrained clairvoyant sees hovering as a cloud in the vicinity of the physical body is the astral body, he is not telling you the truth. For during the night the astral body is poured out over the whole of our solar system. During sleep it comes into connection with the beings of the planets. This is why we call it an 'astral' body. All the other explanations of the term 'astral body' coined in the Middle Ages are wrong. We say 'astral body' because during sleep it has an inner connection with the stars, with the astral world; it is enfolded by it and absorbs its forces.

When you consider this fact, confirmed today by spiritual investigation, you will say to yourselves: 'Then surely the first currents to form this astral body must have come to the human being from the astral world, the world of the stars, and the starry world must have been engaged in earth's becoming.' So when we say that on the fourth 'day' of creation what up till then had been of a soul/spiritual nature clad itself in the laws and forces of the astral body, then on that same fourth 'day' the stars, the *astra*, must have begun their activity in the circumference of the earth.

Genesis confirms this. When on the fourth 'day' we are told about the happening which we can describe as 'the astral body being formed in accordance with its laws', Genesis is giving us an exact parallel of this clothing of the human being, where he still hovers in the spiritual or astral environment of the earth, with the astral body, with the activity of the world of the stars which at that time was part of the earth. Thus here too we find deep meaning which is in complete accord with what clairvoyant investigation can tell us about human beings today. Although we shall realize that at the time of which Genesis speaks the astral body was not the same as our astral body is nowadays during the night, yet its laws were the same and the activity which it developed was the same.

We shall expect that during the next period, which Genesis calls the fifth 'day', a still further densification will take place. Man still remains a supersensible, etheric being, but a further densification does take place in the etheric. Man still does not make contact with the earth, he still belongs to the more spiritual/etheric circumference of the earth; and here we touch on something which is extraordinarily important that we understand for the whole development of man in connection with the earth. When we think about the kingdom next to us human beings, the animal kingdom, we may contemplate a question we have often touched upon before, as to why animals actually became animals and man became man? That man has evolved from the animal kingdom, as crude materialism allows people to think, would not even be accepted by superficial, abstract reasoning if it were to take the matter seriously. If we study the process chronologically and look at the earth's development, we have nevertheless to admit that animals made their appearance before man became visible as an earth being. So that man could become man on earth it was necessary that he met with appropriate conditions for his densification. Suppose that on the fifth 'day' of creation man had become an earthly being such as he is today, that is, that he had become sufficiently densified that he could be called an earthly creature, what would have happened then? He would not have acquired the form nor become the sort of being he has become, for earth conditions were not sufficiently advanced to give man his human form. Humanity had to wait in a spiritual condition, and leave earth to itself, because it could not yet provide the circumstances

for earth existence. Man had first of all to mature in a soul/
spiritual realm, in a more etheric sphere. If he had not waited
with his descent on to the earth he would have become
encased in an animal form. The animals became animals
because the soul/spiritual being, the group soul of these animal forms, descended whilst the earth was not yet ready to
supply the conditions necessary for the earthly human form.
Man had to wait above in a spiritual form. Animals arose
because their inner being descended too early to become
human. At the time of the fifth 'day' the earth consisted of air
and water. Man was not permitted to descend and fashion
himself an earthly body in these. The animals, the group souls
of the animals who did descend, became creatures of the air
and of the water. Thus, while certain group souls were
clothing themselves in bodies suitable for airy and watery
conditions, human beings had to wait in a spiritual form in
order to be able to acquire their human form later.

Genesis describes the whole course of events in a very able
way. What would have happened if on the fifth 'day' man had
already descended into dense matter? The physical part of his
being would not have been able to receive the forces which he
actually did receive through the elohim advancing to become
a unity. We have already spoken of this unifying process of the
elohim, and we have said that Genesis presents it in a most
wonderful way by speaking first of the elohim and later on of
Jehovah-Elohim. We said that the chief characteristic of the
elohim was that they wove in the element of warmth. Warmth
was their element; it was, as it were, the body through which
they manifested themselves. When at the end of the evolutionary series described in Genesis the elohim had progressed
to the point where we can speak of a group consciousness, a
Jehovah-Elohim, there also occurred a change in the nature of
the elohim.

This change followed the same principle as changes in the

other hierarchical beings. You will remember that I spoke of the 'body' of the thrones. We said that at the beginning of our planetary evolution their body was sacrificed to provide the warmth element of ancient Saturn. I then went on to say that we can find the body of the thrones on ancient Sun in the element of air, on ancient Moon in the element of water and during our earthly evolution in the earth or solid element. For the thrones this condensing of their essential being further and further from the state of warmth to that of earth indicated a kind of promotion.

Let us now ask ourselves: If the elohim were to go through a similar advancement, if, as a kind of reward for their work, they were permitted to go up a stage, what would this imply? In accordance with the laws which govern such things, they would have to move on to the next degree of densification. Just as in primordial times, in the transition from ancient Saturn to ancient Sun, the thrones progressed from the element of warmth to that of air, we can expect that the elohim, too, in attaining their unified consciousness will, in regard to their outer manifestation, their outer interaction with a body, progress from the element of warmth to that of air. That, however, did not happen on the fifth 'day' but only at the end of the series of events described in Genesis. Had man been permitted on the fifth 'day' to descend into the finer element of air, the same thing would have happened to him as happened to the other creatures who acquired their bodies in the element of air. They became animals of the air, because they could not be given the strength necessary to lead on to the meaning of earth development, namely the strength of Jehovah-Elohim after the elohim had risen to that stage. Man had therefore to wait. He was not permitted to clad himself in air. When that particular species descended he had to wait until the elohim had become Jehovah-Elohim, for only then could he be given the Jehovah-Elohim strength. He had to become embodied in the weaving substance of Jehovah-Elohim, in the air, but he was not to take this elemental life of the air into himself until he could receive it from Jehovah-Elohim. Genesis has an ingenious way of describing this. It tells us that man continued to develop in a more spiritual/etheric state, and only sought denser embodiment after the elohim had advanced to the stage of Jehovah-Elohim, and Jehovah-Elohim could form the earthly nature of man by breathing the air into him. What streamed into man with the air was the essence of the elohim themselves, having become Jehovah-Elohim.

Here again we have a version in Genesis which accords wonderfully with the findings of spiritual science. In fact in Genesis we find a theory of evolution compared with which the doctrines which people are so proud of today are sheer fantastic dilettantism. For Genesis leads us into the inner sanctuary of creation, showing us what had to happen in the supersensible realm before man could progress to existence in the sense world.

So whilst the other creatures had already condensed physically in the domain of air and water, man had still to remain in an etheric existence, and it was in fact his condensation to the level of the etheric body which took place in the period alluded to as the fifth 'day'. On the fifth 'day' we still do not find man among the physical earth creatures. This did not happen until the sixth 'day'; it was then that he was received by the arising earth, and we can confirm that what we call the human physical body came into existence on what Genesis calls the sixth 'day'.

But we must emphasize that it would be quite wrong if you were to believe that you would have been able to see with your eyes or touch with your hands the human being who came into existence on the sixth 'day'. If it had been at all possible for a person with today's senses to exist at all at that time he would not have been able to perceive the human being who came into existence then. People of today are far too inclined to think materialistically. So when they hear of the sixth 'day' of creation they immediately think of the newly created human being as a being just like themselves. Man was certainly there in physical form, but warmth activity, too, is physical. If you enter a room where there are differentiated currents of warmth not so dense as gas, you must still call them physical; and there was physical existence of this kind as early as the Saturn evolution, even though it was only of the substance of warmth. So it would be wrong to imagine the human being on the sixth 'day' as a creature of flesh. We are justified in expecting him to be a physical earthly being, in fact it is as a physical being that we must look for him, but he existed only in a most delicate manifestation of the physical, as a creature of warmth. When the event occurred so beautifully expressed in the words 'And God said, Let us make man!' a person sensitive to warmth would have perceived certain differentiations in the substance of warmth. If this person had walked on the earth which was at that time covered with the group species of plants and animals in air and water, he might have said to himself: 'Strange things can be perceived. In certain places I get impressions of warmth—not of anything that has reached a gaseous condition—only pure warmth impressions. There are differentiations of warmth in the periphery of the earth. Beings of warmth are flying about.' For the human being was not yet even a gaseous being but only a being of warmth. Think away all the solid part of you, as well as all the fluid part and the gaseous part, and imagine only that part of you which is pulsating in the warmth of your blood. Imagine your blood heat separate from everything else, then you have what came into being as the elohim spoke the creative word: 'Let us make man!' And the next stage of densification came about only after the days of creation. The instreaming of what Jehovah-Elohim was able to give, namely the air, did not take place until the sixth 'day' of creation was over.

Human beings will not understand their own origin until they make up their minds to picture their path of descent in the following order: At the very beginning of earth's creation things were first of all in a soul/spiritual condition, then came the astral, then the etheric, and of the physical conditions there was first of all warmth, and not until after that, air. Even as regards the point of time when, after the six 'days' of creation we are told 'And the Lord God ... breathed into his nostrils the breath of life,' unless we think of man at that moment as consisting only of warmth and air, and do not allow ourselves to believe that he had a fleshly part, we human beings will not understand our own origin. The coarser elements derive from the finer ones, and not vice versa. It goes against the grain for someone with a present-day consciousness to think in this way, yet it is nevertheless true.

When we have grasped this we shall then realize why so many accounts of creation say that the origin of man should be looked at as a descent from the periphery of the earth. When the Bible itself, after telling us about the 'days' of creation, speaks of paradise, here too we must look for a more profound meaning behind it, and only a science of the spirit can put us on the right track. To anyone who knows the truth of the matter, it is really very odd that the commentators should argue as to whether paradise, from which we human beings came, was in this part of the earth or that. It is only too clear in many accounts of creation, including the Bible, that paradise was not on the earth at all, but was raised above the earth's surface, more or less at cloud height,and that while man lived in paradise he was a creature of warmth and air. He most certainly did not walk about on the earth with two legs; that is materialistic day-dreaming. So even after the 'days' of creation were over we have to think of man as a being belonging not on the surface but in the periphery of the earth.

How then did the human being get from the periphery on to the earth; how did the further densification come about from the condition into which Jehovah-Elohim had put man? Here we come to something described pretty fully in my *Outline of Esoteric Science*—to what we call the influence of Lucifer. To express more precisely what we mean by this we must imagine luciferic beings pouring themselves, as it were, into the human astral body, so that the human being, made up as he was of all the forces we have been describing in the earth's becoming, now receives into himself the luciferic influence. We shall understand what this influence signifies if we say that man's life of desire and aspiration, everything anchored in the astral body, became shot through with the luciferic element, became more forceful and passionate, more impelled by greed, more self-centred. To sum up, what we today call egoism, the inclination to be a law unto oneself, the pre-occupation with securing one's own inner comfort, came about through the influence of Lucifer. Everything good or bad which can be classed as a state of inner comfort or satisfaction came from Lucifer. At first it was an alien influence. The astral body as it had been previously, when it was formed by the currents which streamed into it from the world of the stars, now became different, became the kind of astral body which was permeated by the luciferic influence. In consequence the human body of warmth and air became more condensed. It was only now that the man of flesh came into being; it was only now that this further densification occurred. So we can say that the part of the human being belonging to pre-luciferic times is contained in his warmth and air part, and the luciferic influence has insinuated itself into his fluid and solid part. It lives in all that is solid and liquid. And it is not at all a figure of speech but fairly literally describes the situation when I say that, because of the contraction of the human body brought about by the luciferic influence, the human being became heavier and descended out of the periphery on to the surface of the earth. That was the withdrawal from paradise as described in picture form. Not until now did man acquire so to speak the force of gravity to sink down from the periphery on to the earth's surface. This is the descent of man on to the physical earth, what brought him right down to earth, whereas he had hitherto dwelt in its periphery. Therefore the luciferic influence has to be reckoned among the actual formative forces which have fashioned man.

This is why there is such a remarkable parallel between the descriptions derived solely from spiritual scientific investigation and those of the Bible. Please note how in my *Outline of Esoteric Science* I keep clear of anything which might have come about if any part of the Genesis' account had been introduced into it. In my description there I was careful to guard against that. I relied solely on spiritual scientific investigation. Then at a certain point in the account the luciferic influence occurs, decribed here from quite a different aspect. But when we have made this discovery, then in our spiritual scientific description we have reached the very period of time which is described in the Bible as man's temptation by the serpent, by Lucifer. We discovered the parallel later. Just as gravity, elecricity and magnetism are forces which in a coarser way play their part in the formation of our earth today, so too, the development of the earth could not have proceeded without what we call the luciferic influence. We have to include this luciferic influence among the earth-building forces. Oriental accounts of the creation, in particular, but not with such delicacy as those of the Bible, also place paradise in the periphery of the earth and not on the earth itself, and conceive of the expulsion from paradise as a descent from the periphery to the earth's surface. Here also, if we only know how to interpret the words, we find complete agreement between spiritual scientific investigation and the Bible.

But let us now look at another factor. We have stressed the point that things are not so easy for the spiritual investigator as they are for the sort of scientist who works roughly on the principle that 'at night all the cows are grey', and traces any amount of occurrences back to the same underlying cause. Where there is cloud formation the spiritual investigator sees something quite different from what he sees when water forms on the surface of the earth. We have spoken of the cherubim as the directing powers in cloud formation and of the seraphim as the directing powers in the lightning flash that issues from the clouds. If we now look upon the expulsion from paradise as really referring to a descent from the periphery, we are describing almost word for word how man fell through his own weight, and how he had to leave behind him the forces and the beings who form the clouds and the lightning—the cherubim with the flaming sword. Man fell from the earth's periphery out of the region where the cherubim rule with their fiery swords of lightning. There we have a spiritual scientific version that confirms almost word for word the account of the expulsion from paradise according to which the Godhead placed before the gates of paradise the cherubim with the sword of whirling fire. When you realize this, then it becomes almost palpable that those ancient seers who gave us Genesis gazed with full powers of seership into the mysterious processes where the human being moved and had his being in the etheric heights before he fell from the regions where the seraphim and cherubim rule. How realistic the Bible is! Its descriptions are not just similes or crude symbols; they are the direct findings of clairvoyant consciousness.

People of today do not have much of a feeling for the way people in olden times thought about things. The Bible is criticized on all sides for being naïve enough to tell us that paradise was once upon a time a big garden planted with beautiful trees, where lions and tigers roamed around mingling with human beings. It is easy to criticize a description like this, and one flippant critic has gone so far as to ask what would have happened to man if he had been naïve enough to stretch out his hand to one of the lions. Once you have invented a fanciful picture of something never intended by Genesis, then criticism is easy. This kind of outlook has only arisen in recent centuries. People nowadays know very little about the way people of earlier centuries thought. The Scholastics of the twelfth century would be amazed if they were to return today and could hear what they themselves are supposed to have said about the Bible. It would never have occurred to a Scholastic to have the sort of ideas about the Bible such as people have today. People could soon find this out if they really wanted to learn. You only need to study Scholasticism properly to see that they are quite clearly saying that they were talking about something different. Even if there was practically no awareness any longer of the fact that the Bible is a record of clairvoyant investigation, there nevertheless was still something very different there from the crude kind of interpretation that came in with the sixteenth and seventeenth centuries. It would never have occurred to anyone in the early centuries of the Middle Ages to make statements of that sort. Today it is easy to criticize the Bible so long as you ignore the fact that the ideas under attack were only born a few centuries ago. And those who rail against the Bible the most are fighting against a fanciful invention of the human mind and not the Bible. They are fighting against something that does not exist at all, but was imagined in the first place. So it is up to spiritual science, by communicating its findings, to point once more to the true meaning of the Bible, thereby clearing the way for the tremendous impact it is bound to have on us when we come to understand what resounds to us so impressively from ancient times.

Lecture 9, 25 August 1910

The Moon Element in Man

Again and again in these lectures we have been able to show how the Genesis account, rightly interpreted, has corroborated the findings of clairvoyant investigation. However, there remain a number of points still to clear up in this regard. The first thing will be to show with greater precision the point of time at which the Genesis account falls in terms of what spiritual scientific findings tell us with regard to the origin of our earth. I have already referred to this from a certain aspect in that I placed the beginning of Genesis at the time when the sun and earth were about to separate. But we shall have to go into this in greater detail.

Those of you who have heard some of my earlier lectures, and also those who have studied the description of earth evolution in my *Outline of Esoteric Science*, will remember what great importance I attached to two significant moments in this evolution. The first of these is the separation of the sun from the earth. This moment is a very important one. This separation had to take place some time, for had the two cosmic bodies remained united as they were at the beginning of earth existence, the course of human evolution could not have given man his true earthly meaning. All that we include in the term 'sun', obviously not only the elemental or physical constituents in the body of the sun, but also the spiritual beings belonging to it, had to withdraw from the earth or, if you prefer, push the earth out because, if those beings who have transferred their scene of action from the earth to the sun had remained with the earth their forces would have had too strong an effect for man's wellbeing. They had to lessen their forces by removing themselves from the earthly scene and working upon it from outside. So we are concerned with a point of time when, in order to reduce their influences, a number of beings set up their abode outside the earth, and then worked less strongly on the development of both man and animal. From this moment in time onwards the earth is left to itself and, because the finer, the more spiritual forces have withdrawn with the sun, the earth forces undergo a certain coarsening. But man, after the separation of the sun, remained on the earth for a while, still as the being he had become as a result of the Saturn, Sun and Moon stages. It was of course only highly exalted beings who withdrew with the sun and took up their scene of activity outside the earth.

When the earth was left on its own, however, it still had within it all the substances and forces which go to make up the present moon. After the separation of the sun we therefore had an earth evolution which so to speak still had moon evolution within its own body. Man was exposed to conditions which were much coarser than earth conditions proper became later, for the substance of the moon is very coarse. Following on the separation of the sun from the earth, the earth forces therefore became ever more moonlike, ever denser. This then led to humans being exposed to the other danger of dying off, of mummifying astrally. While, so long as the sun remained with the earth, conditions were too refined, they now became too coarse. Consequently, as the development of the earth proceeded, human beings, by maintaining their connection with the earth, were less and less able to thrive. All this is described in detail in my *Outline of Esoteric Science*.

We know from yesterday's lecture that human beings were of course soul/spiritual beings, and for this very reason they could not unite with the earth materiality which rose up into the periphery because, while the moon was still united with the earth, this was too coarse. So it came about that the great majority of human souls had to relinquish their union with the earth. Here we come to something of great importance affecting the relationship between human beings and the earth during the period of time between the departure of the sun and the departure of the moon. Except for a very small number, the soul/spiritual part of human beings took their departure from earth conditions and made their way to higher regions where, according to their level of development, they continued their evolution on the planets belonging to our solar system. Some soul/spirits were more suited to pursue their evolution on Saturn for the time being, others on Mars, others again on Mercury and so on. Only a very small number of the strongest soul/spirits remained connected with the earth, and in the meantime the rest dwelt upon earth's planetary neighbours. This was at a point in time preceding the Lemurian age, to use the customary expression. So what we can call our human soul condition went through an evolution on the neighbouring planets of our earth.

Then came the other important event which took place as we know during the Lemurian age, when the substance of the moon and all its forces was removed from the earth. The moon departed from the earth bringing about great changes in the earth itself. Now, for the first time, the earth came into a condition in which human beings could thrive. Whereas the forces would have been, so to say, too spiritual if the earth had remained united with the sun, they would have had to become too coarse had it remained united with the moon. Therefore the moon also withdrew, and the earth remained behind in a state of balance brought about because sun beings and moon beings both influenced it from outside. The earth prepared itself in this way to be able to be the bearer of human existence. All this happened during the Lemurian age.

Evolution continued, and little by little the human soul/ spirits who had fled to the planets began to return to earth again. This return of the soul/spirits from the neighbouring planets is something that went on for a long time, far into the Atlantean age. Evolution happened in such a way that what had crystallized out as man during the latter part of Lemuria and during Atlantis was gradually endowed with soul/spirits who had different characteristics according to whether they came down from Mars, Mercury or Jupiter and so on. This brought about great variety in man's earthly development. Those of you who are familiar with my last lectures in Christiania will know that this classification into a Mars type, a Saturn type and so on, was the origin of what later became racial differentiation.[1] This is how differences arose among the human race as a whole, and it is still possible today, if you have an eye for it, to recognize whether a person's soul has descended from this or that planet.

But it has also been emphasized—and this has been fully discussed in my *Outline of Esoteric Science*—that by no means all human soul/spirits left the earth. What we might describe as the toughest souls were able to go on using earthly matter, and remain united with it. I have even mentioned that in a surprising way there was a principal human couple who survived the densification of earth. Spiritual investigation impels us to accept what to begin with seems incredible, that there was such a couple as Adam and Eve, as the Bible tells us, and that the races which arose on the return of soul/spirits from the cosmos came about through their union with the descendants of that couple.

If we bear all this in mind then we shall approach an elucidation regarding the point of time in our spiritual scientific chronology to which the Bible account refers. Let me remind you that after the six or seven 'days' of creation have been described there comes what the superficial approach of modern biblical criticism takes for a second, separate account of creation, but which in reality is a perfectly consistent part of it. I would like to remind you of some spiritual scientific results which I have often mentioned, and described in greater detail in my *Outline of Esoteric Science*. I showed how during the advance of earth development from the Lemurian to the Atlantean age a kind of cooling down of the earth took place. During Lemuria we must think of the earth as an entity of an essentially fiery nature, with the element of fire flashing forth all over it; and it was not until the transition to Atlantis that the cooling down process began. During the Atlantean age the atmosphere above the earth's surface was very different from what it became later; a long way into the Atlantean age the earth's atmosphere was still densely humid. The earth was covered with an atmosphere that was totally saturated by something between water and fog. The difference that exists today between whether it is raining or whether the atmosphere is clear of rain did not exist in those ancient times. Everything was shrouded in watery fog, laden with all sorts of fumes and smoke and other substances which had not at that time assumed solid form. Much of what is solid today still streamed through the atmosphere in the form of steam. And everything was pervaded by these masses of watery fog until far into Atlantean times.

But that was the very period when for the first time what had previously existed in a much more spiritual condition began to take on physical form. During the situation as it was on the third 'day' of creation we must not think that the forms of individual plants, as we know them today, sprouted from the earth, but that we must give full weight to the phrase 'after his kind', meaning that the reference is rather to the souls of species which were present in the body of the earth in etheric/ astral form. What was described on the third 'day' as the creation of plants would not have been visible to outer senses but only to clairvoyant organs of perception. During the time lasting from the end of Lemuria right on into Atlantis, when the condition of fog developed in the periphery of the earth and then gradually thinned, what had previously been of an etheric nature became transformed into a condition somewhat resembling what we know today. What had been etheric became more and more physical. It may sound strange today—particularly as geology is largely pervaded by materialistic viewpoints—but the kind of plant kingdom visible to the external eye did not come into existense until much later than the time indicated in the account of the third 'day' of creation. It did not come about until the time of Atlantis. The geological conditions necessary for today's plants must not be ascribed to these very early times in our investigation.

The course of events from the end of Lemuria on into Atlantean times could be characterized as follows: The earth was covered by dense volumes of fog, in which the various substances later to be transformed into the crust of the earth were still in the form of smoke, and the beings of species visible to clairvoyant consciousness had not yet achieved physical densification. The fertilizing of the earth's surface with the water hovering in the air had not yet taken place: that only happened later. How could the Bible give the first mention of this? It would have to say at a definite point: 'Even after the conclusion of the seven days of creation, after what coincides with the Lemurian age had taken place, still none of the plants we know today sprouted from the earth, and the earth was still covered with fog.'

The Bible does in fact say this. If you read on after the seven 'days' of creation you find it mentioned that there were still no herbaceous plants or shrubs on the earth, although it had been said earlier that the plant forms had arisen as species. On the first occasion the reference was to souls of the species, and the second time to something which sprang from the earth as vegetation in individual physical form. The Atlantean fog is described as in fact it was after the 'days' of creation. The words 'For the Lord God had not caused it to rain upon the earth' indicate that it was only after the 'days' of creation that the condensation of the water in the atmosphere to rain came about.

There is deep wisdom hidden here. But I can assure you that nothing from this document influenced the description I gave in *An Outline of Esoteric Science*. I purposely refrained from consulting the Bible, and there were times, I might say, when I had to try very hard to reach these things in a different way than from this ancient document. Modern materialistic ideas of the Bible make it inevitable that one should not readily read into it any of the facts of spiritual science. But spiritual science compelled us to find in the Bible what we have been able to say in these lectures, and despite our own reluctance we have been obliged at last to recognize in the Bible what clairvoyant investigation had previously discovered.

Having sorted this out we may now go on to ask where in the Genesis account do we have to place the departure of human spirit/souls to the neighbouring planetary bodies or planetary beings caused by the hardening condition of the earth. We have to put it at the point where it says that through the formation of the sound ether the upper substances are separated from the lower ones. I went into that fully in my description of the second 'day'. If you follow all this with the eye of a seer you realize that along with what withdrew from the earth, which the elohim called 'heaven', there withdrew at the same time the soul/spirits of human beings. Therefore the second 'day' of creation coincides with a specific period between the withdrawal of the sun and the withdrawal of the moon.

However, we must bear in mind that this had a very

important follow-up. What exactly was it that went out into the cosmos at that time? In other words, where do we find it today in human beings? In which members of the human being do we expect to locate it? Of course it does not exist today in the form it had in those times, but we can nevertheless find something corresponding to it in a certain part of our present human organization. Let us have a look at the human being with that in mind. Nowadays we distinguish in the human being the four familiar members: The physical, etheric and astral bodies and the bearer of the ego. We know that during sleep the physical and etheric bodies remain in bed. When we are concerned with those ancient times which apply to the second 'day' of creation and even the third as well, we should not speak of physical and etheric bodies as we know them today. These were only formed out of earth substance later. All there was of the human being at that time belonged to what nowadays withdraws from the coarser members of his being, what we call his astral being. It is the forces at work in our astral body that we must have in mind when we think of the human soul/spirit which took leave of the earth at that time in order to thrive better on the surrounding planets. It is all that belongs to our forces when our astral body is outside our physical and etheric bodies that we have to expect to find on the surrounding planets after the second 'day'.

We know, however, that when nowadays the human being, in the state of sleep, is outside his physical and etheric bodies, he becomes part of the astral environment of our earth, of the forces and currents of the members of our planetary system. During sleep human beings are in connection with planetary beings. So we can say that in those ancient times human beings were not only united with these planets outside during sleep, but after this flight from the earth they were united with them all the time. They stayed there. Therefore we have to bear in mind that during the third 'day' of creation human soul/spirits—with the exception of those I mentioned who survived earth conditions—were not on the earth at all, but they settled on the planets surrounding the earth and underwent further development there. In the meantime the strongest, toughest human soul/spirits continued developing on earth, and their development consisted in clothing themselves more and more with earthly material, so that there below on the earth the first models were coming into being of the etheric and physical bodies we now live in during the day. It was in order that these etheric and physical bodies should be able to play their part in every situation of earth evolution that some of the soul/spirits were kept alive on earth. By that means the etheric and physical bodies which were in the process of being prepared were propagated even while the moon forces were still united with the earth.

If we take a really good look at the state of things after the separation of the sun we have to say that most of the substance of human soul/spiritual nature was in the periphery of the earth on the neighbouring planets. The sun had already departed from the earth, but if a human being had been able to station himself on the earth at that time he would have seen upon its surface dense masses of a mixture of fog, smoke and steam. He would have seen no trace of the sun. The sun's forces were far away, and only little by little did they begin to have the effect on earth of clearing up the masses of smoky fog and bringing the atmosphere into a condition necessary for human evolution. Our imaginary person, looking at evolution from outside, would have seen that it was only very gradually that the fog began to clear and the volumes of smoke to thin out; and the forces of the sun now began no longer to work their way through a dark covering of smoke but to be perceptible, actually visible. We are now approaching the fourth 'day' and getting closer and closer to the event we call the separation of the moon. So our imaginary human being would actually have caught sight of the rays of the sun penetrating through the volumes of smoke and steam, and while this was happening the earth gradually assumed a condition favourable to human development, so that human beings could once again live on earth. The physical descendants of those who had survived in earth bodies could now provide bodies for the soul/spirits who began to return from the periphery of the earth.

So we have two kinds of propagation. What later became human etheric and physical bodies were passed down by those who had remained on earth. The soul/spiritual part comes in from the periphery of the earth. To begin with this arrival from the circles of the planetary neighbours of our earth was a spiritual influence. At the moment when the sun had penetrated the clouds of steam and smoke in the earth's atmosphere and the moon had departed, there awoke in the soul/spirits on the planets the urge to come down again into the earthly realm. When on the one hand the sun became visible on the earth and on the other hand also the moon, that was the time when the forces of the souls streaming down to earth entered the earthly sphere. This is the reality behind the words used to describe the fourth 'day' of creation: 'And God made two great lights; the greater light to rule the day, and the lesser light to rule the night: he made the stars also.' For the stars actually mean the planetary neighbours of our earth. The creative deed which brought about a kind of balance was set going on the one hand by the sun and on the other by the moon, and at the same time the human soul/spirits who were seeking to reincarnate on earth began to exert their influence.

This places the fourth 'day' of creation at a point in the Lemurian age when, after the exit of the moon, those conditions came about which you find described in my *Outline of*

Esoteric Science, and which we can sum up in the words: 'The human soul/spirits are seeking to return again to earth.'

But now we must give a little thought to the accompanying spiritual conditions. We have just been looking more at what was heading towards becoming physical. We must realize more and more clearly that everything coarse has a refined element behind it and everything that is moving towards becoming physical has a spiritual side. With the exit of the sun the elohim, in the main, left the earth to set up their scene of action outside it so as to be able to influence it from the periphery. But not all of them went. A part of the elohim remained united with the earth even while the earth still had the moon forces within it. Part of the spiritual forces of the elohim remained united with the earth, that part which in a way is bound up with all the good effects of the moon forces. For we must speak of good moon influences, too. After the separation of the sun everything on earth, especially human beings, would have been driven into a state of mummification, of hardening. The human being would have been lost to the earth. The earth would have become a desert waste if it had retained the moon forces within it. *Within* the earth the moon forces would never have been beneficial. Why was it, then, that they had still to remain on earth for a while? As humankind had to endure every kind of earth condition its toughest representatives actually had to go through this moon densification. But when the moon had departed from the earth its forces, which otherwise would have led to the death of the earth, became beneficial. After the withdrawal of the moon forces everything revived again, so that even the weaker souls could descend and incarnate in human bodies. Therefore by becoming its neighbour, the moon became earth's benefactor—which from within the earth it never could have been. The beings who directed this whole series of events are the great benefactors of humankind. Which beings were these? They were the very beings who had just united themselves with the moon and who then as it were tore the moon out of the earth in order to guide humankind further in earth evolution. We recognize from the Genesis account that the elohim were the great directing forces. And the elohim forces which brought about the mighty event of the moon's withdrawal, and thereby enabled human beings to assume their proper nature, were none other than the very forces which brought about the cosmic advancement of the elohim to Jehovah-Elohim. This unified group remained united with the moon and was what drew it out of the earth. Therefore we can conclude that what we call Jehovah-Elohim is intimately connected with what we know as the body of the moon within the created world.

Let us now picture to ourselves more exactly what these circumstances actually signify for man on earth. If the human being had remained bound to an earth which had retained the sun within it he would have become a nothing; he would have simply remained attached to the umbilical cord of the elohim, and would not have been able to sever this bond and attain his independence. But because the elohim withdrew from the earth with the sun, human beings could remain with the earth and maintain their life of soul and spirit. If things had stopped there, however, human beings would have become hardened and found their death. Why did human beings have to reach a condition which provided even the possibility of dying off? So that they could become free, cut themselves off from the elohim and acquire independent being. In his moon part the human being has something within him which actually causes this dying off, and he would have had too large a dose of it if the moon had not separated from the earth. But you will see that it follows that it is the very moon element which, as a cosmic substance, is intimately connected with human independence.

If you look at present conditions on earth you must realize that these actually only came about after the moon separation. So there is not so much moon activity left in the present state of things as there used to be. As far as the foundations of his physical and etheric bodies are concerned, however, man has survived the period when the earth was united with the moon, and therefore he has within him something of what was taken from the earth and is now up there on the moon. He has retained it in his physical and etheric bodies ever since. Therefore man has a bit of moon nature in him, and this is how he made his connection with it. The earth could not have stood having this moon element within it, but in a certain way man has it in him. He has the disposition to be something more than only an earth being.

If you think about all this then you realize that as human beings we so to speak have the earth beneath us, and that the moon had to be cast out of this earth. But it was not thrown out until the right dose of its nature had been inoculated into man himself. The *earth* does not contain any moon nature in it; it is we who have it in us. What would have become of the earth if the moon had not been torn out of it? Look at the moon for a moment with rather different eyes, the way people so often do today. Its whole material constitution is different from that of the earth. From a grossly material aspect the astrophysicist says that the moon has no air and scarcely any water, i.e. that it is far denser than the earth; meaning that it contains forces which would have brought the earth beyond the condition of densification which it actually has, and made it physically even harder than it is. The moon forces would make the earth physically harder, more fissured than it is. To have a picture of what the earth would become if the moon forces were in it, think of a wet and muddy lane becoming dustier and dustier as the water in it evaporates. You can see the whole process happening when after a fall of rain the mud in the lane gradually turns to dust. Something like that would have happened to the earth on a large scale if the moon forces had remained within it—it would have cracked and crumbled into lumps of dust. Something like this *will* happen to the earth some day when it has fulfilled its task—it will crumble into cosmic dust. Earthly matter will dissolve as cosmic dust into cosmic space when man has finished evolving upon it.

We can say, then, that the earth would have become dust, that it had the tendency to become dust, to crumble into particles of dust. It has only been saved from doing so too soon by the withdrawal of the moon. But in man something has remained of the disposition to become dust. Through the situation I have described to you man received into his being something of this moonlike earth dust. Those beings connected with the moon actually introduced into man's bodily nature something which is basically not of the earth as it is after the separation of the moon—and as we experience it in our immediate surroundings; they have imprinted into the human body something of the moonlike earth dust. However, as Jehovah-Elohim is connected with this moon nature, it means that it is Jehovah-Elohim who has imprinted this moonlike earth dust into the human body. So there must have been a point in the course of earth evolution of which it would be correct to say that during the cosmic advancement of the elohim Jehovah-Elohim imprinted earth dust into the human body, moonlike earth dust. This is the tremendously profound meaning in the passage in the Bible which says that Jehovah-Elohim formed man of the dust of the earth. For that is what it says. None of the translations which convey that Jehovah-Elohim formed man out of 'a clod of earth' make any sense. What Jehovah-Elohim did was imprint earth dust into man.

Not a few of the startling discoveries we have already made have filled us with such awestruck veneration in regard to the revelations uttered in the Bible by the ancient seers and rediscovered in our own day by spiritual scientific research. But here, with the words 'And Jehovah-Elohim imprinted into man's bodily nature the moonlike earth dust', the account given by the clairvoyant authors of Genesis may well inspire in us a sensation of almost overwhelming reverence. If those ancient seers were aware that the inspiration to which they gave utterance came to them out of the very regions where the elohim and Jehovah-Elohim were active—if they were consciously receiving their wisdom from the realms of the world creators themselves, then they could say: 'What streams into us in the form of knowledge, wisdom, thought, is of the essence of that which, through its creative activity, formed the living being of the earth.' Therefore we can look up in holy awe to those ancient seers who themselves, in holy awe, looked up into those regions from which they received their inspiration, the realm of the elohim and Jehovah-Elohim. What name could they have given to those beings who underpinned both the creation and their own knowledge of it? What kind of word could there be for them unless it were one that conveyed the full force of their hearts on receiving this revelation from the powers that created the world? Looking up to these beings, they said to themselves: 'This revelation flows down to us from divine/spiritual beings. We can find no other word for them than the one that expresses our feeling of holy awe.' If we translate that into ancient Hebrew, what does it sound like? 'Those for whom we feel holy awe—*elohim!* This is the Hebrew word for those beings for whom man feels holy awe.' Here you have the link between the feelings of the ancient seers and the name of those cosmic beings to whom they attributed both the creation and the revelation they received.

The Way the Bible Accords with Clairvoyant Research

From all that has been said in the last few days, and especially yesterday, you will have been able to gather at about what point in time of our spiritual scientific description we have to place Genesis. In fact we have pointed out that the first monumental words of the Bible mark the moment when we should say in terms of spiritual science that the substance which is still that of a united earth/sun is making ready to separate. Then follows the separation, and during this whole process that which is described in the opening passages of Genesis takes place. The Genesis account covers all that happens right into the Lemurian age, up to the separation of the moon. And what is described by spiritual science as coming after the withdrawal of the moon, namely the age of Lemuria and the beginning of the Atlantean age, is to be found in the description following on after the 'days' of creation. We mentioned this yesterday. We also referred to the profound meaning in the statement that man's body was imprinted with the dust of earth/moon. This was at the same point in time as the ascent in the cosmos which we called the cosmic advancement of the elohim to become Jehovah-Elohim. We were to think of this advancement as more or less coinciding with the beginning of the moon's activity from outside. We must make sure we think of the activity of the moon, i.e. of the beings who were connected with the process of the moon's withdrawal and therefore of the moon's activity from outside, as being associated with the totality of the elohim, with what we call Jehovah-Elohim. So we can say: The effect of the moon on the earth in its first stage corresponds with everything coming under the heading of the imprinting of the dust of the moonlike earth matter into the human body. The human body, which up to this point had consisted solely of warmth, is given what is usually translated in the words: 'And the Lord God ... breathed into his nostrils the breath of life; and man became a living soul'—or, to put it better, a living being.

We must not fail to notice the aptness, the grandeur, the power of the biblical words. I have impressed upon you that the moment of actually becoming earthly man depended on his being permitted to remain spiritually in a spiritual state until suitable conditions were present in the developing earth itself; through the postponement of taking on flesh he was able to become mature. If he had had to descend sooner from his spiritual state to a bodily one, let us say during the processes indicated by the fifth 'day', he could only have become a being physically resembling the creatures described as living in the regions of air and water. How does Genesis actually describe this essential nature of man? Wonderfully! The passage is a model of accurate and appropriate wording. We are told that the creatures, that is, the group souls who descended into earth matter on the fifth 'day', became living creatures—what we actually call living creatures today. Man did not descend as yet. The group souls who were still as it were in the great reservoir of the spirit world did not descend until later. And when the sixth 'day' came it was first of all the animals closest to man, the earthly animals proper, who came down. So even during the first part of the sixth 'day' man was not permitted to descend into solid matter, for if he had imprinted into himself at that time the forces of the developing earth then physically he would have become a creature resembling the earthly animals. The group souls of the higher animals descended first and populated the earth as distinct from the air and the water. Only after that did the conditions gradually arise favourable to the formation of the prototype of humankind.

How was it achieved? It is conveyed to us in momentous words, where we are told that the beings of the elohim set about combining their activities in order to form man according to the image I described to you. So we have to say: Earth man arose first of all because the elohim, each with a different capacity, worked together as a group to achieve a common purpose. Man began by being the common goal of the elohim as a group.

We must try to get a closer picture of what man was actually like on the sixth 'day'. He was of course not yet like he is today. The physical body which man inhabits today only arose later when Jehovah-Elohim breathed into man the living breath. The event which is described as the creation of man by the elohim took place before earthly dust had been imprinted into the human body. So what was he like, this human being whom the elohim brought into existence as early as the so-called Lemurian age?

Remember what I have often said about the essential nature of a present-day person. From a certain point of view all human beings are the same only with respect to their higher members. With regard to their sex they are different in that males have a feminine etheric body and females a masculine etheric body. This is how our humanity is divided up nowadays. What appears as masculine externally is feminine inside, and what appears feminine externally is masculine inside. How did this come about? At a relatively late time, after the actual 'days' of creation, a differentiation occurred in the human body. In the human being who arose on the sixth 'day' of creation as the common goal of the elohim, there was no such differentiation as the separation into man and woman.

At that time human beings still had the same kind of body. We can describe it best, as far as we can imagine it at all, by saying that the physical body was more etheric still, whereas the etheric body was somewhat denser than today. In other words, what is our dense physical body today was not as dense at the time it was formed by the elohim, and the etheric body was denser than today. A densification towards becoming more physical only occurred later under the influence of Jehovah-Elohim. So you will appreciate that we do not have any reason to speak of the elohim's creation of man as male and female in today's sense, but that it was both male and female at the same time, not yet differentiated. The human being, therefore, who arose when the Bible tells us the elohim said 'Let us make man' was not differentiated as yet, but was both male and female, and through this creation of the elohim man came into being male-female. This is the meaning, the original meaning of the words translated so grotesquely in modern Bibles, 'Male and female created he them.' This does not refer to male and female in today's sense, but to the undifferentiated human being, the male-female human being.

I am well aware that numerous biblical commentators have objected to this interpretation, and with a kind of learned boasting have sought to ridicule the truth of what earlier extremely wise commentators have already said on the subject. They try to discard the view that the elohim's human being was at one and the same time male-female, and that this male-female human being was what was created in the image of the elohim. I should like to ask such commentators what they base their argument on. It cannot be on clairvoyant investigation, for that will never say anything other than what I have just told you. If they rely on external research I should like to ask them how, in face of tradition, they justify any other interpretation. One ought at least to tell people what the biblical tradition is. When through clairvoyant research we first discover the true facts then these Bible texts are filled with life and light, and minor discrepancies in tradition no longer matter, because knowledge of the truth enables us to read the text correctly. But it is a different matter if we approach these things from the standpoint of philology. We should realize that right into Christian times there was nothing even in the first chapters of the Bible to mislead anyone into reading the text as it is read today. There were no vowels in it at all, and the text still had to be broken down into separate words. The punctuations which in Hebrew signify the vowels were only inserted later. Without being prepared by spiritual science, what right has anyone to offer an interpretation of the original text of which he can say, on the basis of scholarship and conscience, that it is reliable?

So where the elohim's creation of man is concerned we should see it as a preparatory stage of human existence. All the processes coming under the heading of 'human propagation' were at that time more etheric, more spiritual; they were on a higher level, one could almost say on a higher plane. It was the activity of Jehovah-Elohim which first made man into what he has become today. That had to be preceded by the systematic creation of the other, lower creatures. Thus this latter creation became living creatures by what one might call a premature act of creation. The same expression *nefesh*,[1] living creature, is applied to these animals and is ultimately applied to man.[2] But how is it applied to man? At the moment when Jehovah-Elohim comes on the scene and makes man into the man of today, we are told emphatically that Jehovah-Elohim imprints man with *neshama*.[3] It is through having a higher member imprinted into him that this same man became a living being.

Note what an immensely significant and fertile concept is introduced into the theory of evolution by the Bible itself! It would be foolish in the extreme not to recognize that, as regards his external form, man belongs at the peak of animal creation. This small concession may be made to Darwinism. But the essential thing is that man did not become a living creature in the same way as the other, lower creatures, whose nature is described as *nefesh*, but that man had first to be given a higher member which had already been prepared in the soul/ spiritual realm.

Here we meet with another parallel between the ancient Hebrew doctrine and our spiritual science. When we speak of human soul qualities we distinguish between sentient soul, intellectual soul and consciousness soul. We know that initially these arose, in their soul/spiritual form, during the first three 'days' of creation. That was when they were first designed. But the incorporating of these—the imprinting of these in a physical body which became the expression of the actual inner essence of man's soul being, happened much later. What we have to hang on to is that the spiritual part arose first, then this is first of all clothed in an astral part and then condenses stage by stage to the etheric/physical level, and that not until then is the spiritual imprinted into it—what had been created earlier is imprinted into the body as the breath of life. Thus what was implanted as a seed into the human being by Jehovah-Elohim had already been formed earlier. It was there in the womb of the elohim. Now it is imprinted into man whose bodily nature had been built up from another direction. So it was something that came through another stream. And with this imprinting of *neshama* it now became possible to give to man the potential to become an ego. For these old Hebrew expressions *nefesh, ruach, neshama*, are none other than what we have described as corresponding to our spiritual scientific terms of sentient soul, intellectual soul and consciousness soul.

We have to realize that the stages of this evolution form an extremely complicated process. We have to think of every-thing to do with the 'days' of creation, everything that is the work of the elohim before they advanced to Jehovah-Elohim, as having taken place in higher, spiritual realms, and what we can observe physically today in the human world did not arise until Jehovah-Elohim began to be active.

Everything we find in the Bible, and again now through clairvoyant perception—without which we should have no understanding of man's actual inner nature—all this was kept alive in the consciousness of Greek philosophers through their initiation centres. This was especially the case with Plato, but also even with Aristotle. Anyone familiar with the works of Plato and Aristotle knows that there was still an awareness that man first became a living being through the introduction of a higher soul/spiritual member, whereas the lower creatures went through different evolutionary processes. Aristotle expressed it somewhat as follows. He said that the lower animals became what they were through other processes of evolution; but that at the time when the forces which are active in the animals were able to become effective the soul/ spiritual being of man, which still hovered in higher regions, was not yet permitted to acquire an earthly body, otherwise it would have remained at the animal stage. The being of man had to wait, and in him the lower, animal stages had to be ousted from their sovereignty through the implanting of the human member. To express this, Aristotle made use of the word *phtheiresthai*.[4] What he meant by this was, 'Of course, superficially speaking, man has the same bodily functions as animals, yet in the animal these functions are supreme, whereas in man the bodily functions have been dethroned and have to follow a higher principle.' This is what *phtheiresthai* means.

The same truth lives behind the biblical story of creation. Through the implanting of *neshama* the lower members were dethroned. With the bearer of his ego man has acquired a higher member. But his earlier, more etheric nature thereby became differentiated downwards. Man acquired an external bodily member and an inner, more etheric member, the one becoming denser and the other more rarefied. The same principle was repeated in man which we have come to recognize as running through the whole of evolution. We saw warmth being condensed to air and rarefied to light, air being condensed to water and rarefied to sound ether and so on. The same process takes place on higher levels in man. The masculine/feminine element became differentiated into man and woman, and further, the denser physical body moved to the outside and the more rarefied etheric body, in an invisible condition, to the inside. We could also call this a reference to the progress from the creation of the elohim to the creation of Jehovah-Elohim. The human being we know today is the creation of Jehovah-Elohim, and the sixth 'day' therefore corresponds to our Lemurian age in which we speak of the male/female human being.

The Bible also speaks of a seventh 'day', and we are told that on this seventh 'day' the elohim ceased their work. What does this actually mean? How are we to understand this further episode? We only grasp it properly from a spiritual scientific point of view when we realize that this is the very moment when the elohim go through their advancement to Jehovah-Elohim. But we must not think of Jehovah-Elohim as being the whole hierarchy of the elohim, but rather that the elohim send only part of their being to the moon and hold the rest in reserve, and continue their own further evolution in this established part of their being. This means that as far as this part of them is concerned their work is no longer devoted to the nurturing of man, and they only work further on mankind with the part of their being which has become Jehovah-Elohim. The other part does not work directly upon the earth but devotes itself to its own evolution. This is what is meant by 'resting' from working with earthly matters, by the sabbath day, the seventh 'day'.

We must now call attention to something else of importance. If everything I have just been saying is correct then we must regard the Jehovah human being, the human being into whom Jehovah impressed his own being, as the direct successor of the more etheric, more delicate human being who was created on the sixth 'day'. So there is a direct line from the more etheric human being, the being who is still male-female, to the physical human being. This physical human being is the descendant, so to say, a densified form of the etheric human being. And if you wanted to describe the Jehovah human being who passes over to Atlantis you would have to say that the human being who was created by the elohim on the sixth 'day' evolved into the unisexual human being, the Jehovah human being. Those who followed after the seven 'days' of creation are the descendants of the elohim human beings, of what came into being altogether during the six 'days' of creation. Again the Bible is magnificent when, in the second chapter, it tells us that the Jehovah human being is in fact a descendant of the heavenly human being, the human being who was created by the elohim on the sixth 'day'. The Jehovah human being is the descendant of the elohim human being in precisely the same way as the son is the descendant of his father. The Bible tells us this in the fourth verse of the second chapter when it says that those who are to follow are the descendants, the subsequent generations of the heavenly human being.

This is what it really says. But if you take a modern translation you find the strange sentence: 'These are the generations of the heavens and of the earth when they were created, in the day that the Lord God made the earth and the heavens.' Usually the whole hierarchy of the elohim is called 'God' and the Jehovah-Elohim is called 'the Lord God'—'The Lord God made the earth and the heavens.' I ask you please to look at this sentence carefully and try honestly to find a reasonable meaning in it. I would be glad to know if anyone can! Anyone who claims to do so had better not look on ahead in his Bible, for the word used here is *toldot*,[5] which means 'subsequent generations', the same expression as is used when the subsequent generations of Noah are being discussed.[6] It is speaking here of the Jehovah human beings as the descendants, the subsequent generations of heavenly beings, in exactly the same way as it speaks there of the descendants of Noah. So this passage should read something like this: 'In what follows we are speaking of the descendants of the beings of heaven and earth who were created by the elohim and whose development was continued by Jehovah-Elohim.'

Therefore the Bible, too, looks upon the Jehovah human beings as the descendants of the elohim human beings. Anyone who wants to presuppose a fresh account of the creation because it says that God created man should also look at the fifth chapter which usually begins: 'This is the book of the generations' (the word used there is the same one as in the other passage: *toldot*). Such a person might as well consider this a third account, thus making his rainbow Bible complete! Then you will have a Bible which is a compilation of separate fragments, but not a real Bible. If we could spend more time on this we would be able to elucidate what is said in chapter five, too.

We see, then, when we go deeply into these things, that there is full agreement between the biblical account of the creation and what we can establish through spiritual or esoteric science. This leads us to ask why the Bible account is in a more or less pictorial form. What do these descriptions represent? They make us realize that they, too, are the result of clairvoyant experience! Just as today the eye of the seer gazes into the supersensible realm, upon the origin of our earthly existence, so too did those who originally composed the Bible story gaze into the supersensible realm. It was by clairvoyant experience that the facts originally given to us were acquired. When we set to work to construct prehistory from the point of view of purely physical observation we start from the traces of it which are extant and discoverable by external means. And the further back we go in physical life and physical origins the more hazy the forms become. But in this misty element spiritual beings are active, and the human being himself in his spiritual part was originally within them. If we pursue our study of the earth's creation as far back as the times Genesis is talking about, our earth merges with these primordial spiritual conditions. The 'days' of creation refer to spiritual processes of development to be grasped only by spiritual investigation. What the Bible is telling us is that physical conditions form gradually out of spiritual conditions.

This is how clairvoyant perception presents evolution. When the seer gazes upon the facts described to us in Genesis he finds at first only spiritual processes. Everything described there is a spiritual process. A physical eye would see absolutely nothing; it would gaze into a void. But, as we have seen, time moves on. Little by little clairvoyant perception sees the solid element crystallize out of spirit, in the same way as ice forms and solidifies out of water. Out of the flowing sea of the astral, of the devachanic world, there emerge the shapes and forms which can now also be seen by the physical eye. That is, in the further course of clairvoyant observation, within the pictures which can initially only be grasped spiritually, physical existence emerges like a crystallization. Therefore it follows that at an earlier time physical eyes would not have been able to discover the human being. Right up to the sixth and seventh 'days' of creation, that is, right up to our Lemurian age, man could not have been seen by the physical eye, for he only existed spiritually. That is the great difference between a true theory of evolution and a trumped up one. The latter assumes that physical development is all there is. But man did not arise through lower creatures progressing to acquire human form. It is incredible that people can think that an animal form turned into the higher form of a human being. Whilst these animal forms were arising, forming their physical bodies below, man had already existed for a long time, but it was only later that he descended and took his place beside the animals. Anyone who cannot look upon evolution in this way is beyond help; he is hypnotized, as it were, by modern concepts, not by scientific facts but by contemporary opinion.

If we want to describe man in relation to the rest of creation we have to say that in the evolutionary process the birds and marine creatures arose as two separate branches, and then, as a special offshoot, the land animals. The former would correspond to the fifth 'day' and the latter to the sixth 'day' of creation. Only then did man appear; though not by continuing the series but by descending to earth. This is the true version of evolution, and it is contained more exactly in the Bible than in any modern textbook which succumbs to materialistic fantasy.

These are just a few fragmentary remarks such as always seem to be required in the last lecture of a series. To follow up adequately every aspect of such a theme as this would take months, for there is such a tremendous amount in Genesis. All that these lectures can do is plant seeds—get you going—and that is all I have attempted to do this time. I would like to give special emphasis to the fact that it was not especially easy for me to give this particular course of lectures. For it is no easy matter for someone who has been attending them to realize how difficult it is to reach the deeper foundations of the biblical story of creation, and to find the parallel between already ascertained spiritual facts and the corresponding passages in the Bible. If one works conscientiously the task is an extremely exacting one. It is often assumed that the eye of the seer can reach whatever it wants to see, that you only have to look, and everything comes by itself. An inexperienced person often thinks he can explain everything easily. But the further you probe, the more numerous the difficulties become. This is so even in ordinary external research, but when you go as far as stepping beyond physical research into the clairvoyant realm, then you are into real difficulties, and along with them comes the awareness of the great responsibility incurred if you want to open your mouth about these things at all. Nevertheless I believe I may say that I have not made use of a single word in these lectures which, as far as it goes in our language, is not an adequate expression which can lead to the right picture. But it was not easy.

You know, the intention was there to ask our dear friend Herr Seiling to give a report, at the beginning or end of these lectures, about the seven days of creation, and to do it in his artistic way of speaking of which we had an example yesterday.[7] You will easily understand how impossible it would have been to have the usual texts spoken, especially as we had been searching for an adequate way to express what is actually being said in Genesis. And there was a very faint hope that perhaps at the end of today something in the nature of an interpretation acquired through spiritual research might have been presented. But with the large invasion of visitors over the last few days we could not possibly venture even to attempt to put together an interpretation of Genesis which would be fit to present. It would not have been the right thing to try, and we must put it off until later. For the time being we shall have to be satisfied with the brief indications you can glean from the lectures. For I assure you that I consider a real interpretation to be a task which requires about a hundred times as much mental effort as I had to apply for our mystery play right from the moment of its first conception to the final step, the performing of it. Anyone who knows the difficulties will find the producing of a decent text of Genesis a hundred times more exacting than what we were endeavouring to achieve with the mystery play which in itself was no easy feat, either. It is precisely when we tackle what are presented to us as the world's great mysteries that the difficulties pile up, and it is a good thing to be aware of this fact, because it is in recognizing and accepting these difficulties that we shall make progress in a right understanding of things anthroposophical.

Our anthroposophical attitude must be one of broad-mindedness towards everything and everyone who should be co-operating so that anthroposophical activity can come about. Therefore, although we have our own definite working methods, we must on no account regard any other working method as not being suitable for us. Civilization today, in fact the whole spiritual/cultural evolution of our times, necessitates different ways of arriving at one and the same goal. And even if it is not my province at all to come before you in any other way than as working out of esotericism, you will never find that I exclude another working method. I have particular reason to mention this at the end of these lectures, where we were led through the help of esotericism to such sublime heights of anthroposophical research. With this in mind I would like to point out what a good thing it is if you can receive help from every direction in support of the anthroposophical point of view, and if you can also acquaint yourselves with what links up with our esotericism from other types of research. With this in mind—and so as to be all-embracing in this area—I would like to draw your attention to the positive good of a book written by our dear friend Herr Ludwig Deinhard, which brings together so satisfactorily the kind of things which can be useful to us in investigations made in other ways.[8] And as a good, harmonious relationship has been sought for and demonstrated, particularly in respect of our kind of esotericism, this presentation cannot be anything else but beneficial even to us anthroposophists. You will find a number of things in it which can be useful to you on the anthroposophical path.

I could mention many more things. I want to make sure to mention a second thing, something which has been borne in upon us at every stage in these lectures—namely how essential it is that in our hearts and imaginations anthroposophical knowledge should grow into something that is so inspiring to our inner life that we are raised to ever higher forms of perception and feeling, to ever more broadminded and vital ways of understanding the world. It all depends on whether we become better people in regard to our intellect, perceptiveness and morality, for that is the touchstone for the fruitfulness of what we can get in the spiritual scientific field. To study the parallel between spiritual scientific investigation and the Bible can be particularly fruitful; for it gives us the rare opportunity to experience that we have our primordial cause, our 'primordial state', as Jakob Boehme would have said,[9] in that supersensible, spiritual womb whence also came those very elohim who rose to becoming Jehovah-Elohim, to that higher evolutionary form, so that they could bring about the great goal of their creative activity, which we call man. Let us approach our origin with due reverence, but also with a due sense of responsibility. The elohim and Jehovah-Elohim gave of their greatest forces to set our evolution going. Let us regard our origin as laying upon us an obligation to our humanhood to take into ourselves more and more of the spiritual forces which, in the course of subsequent evolution, have entered into earth becoming.

We have spoken of the influence of Lucifer. Because of this influence, a part of what lay in the womb of that spirituality in which man, too, originated remained behind in the lap of the gods, and appeared later in the incarnation of the Christ in the body of Jesus of Nazareth. Since that time Christ has been active in earth development as a second divine principle.

Contemplation of the great truths of Genesis ought to point us to the duty of taking up increasingly into our own being the spiritual being of the Christ. For only by filling ourselves with the Christ principle shall we fulfil our whole task as human beings, and become on earth more and more like what we were predisposed to be in those times indicated in the biblical story of creation (told in Genesis).

Therefore a lecture series such as this cannot only give us knowledge but can stir forces to life in our souls. Even if we forget some of the details, may what we have learnt from looking more closely at Genesis work further as soul force. I may perhaps be permitted to say at the close of these few days during which we have been trying again to immerse ourselves deeply for a short while in the stream of anthroposophical life: Let us try to take from these thoughts we have acquired the forces which they ought to engender! Let us carry them forth, and let us fructify by means of these forces our life in the outside world. Whatever we may be doing in life, whatever secular vocation we may have, these forces can be a beacon light for our actions, and can both fructify our activities and enhance our joy and happiness. And no-one who has understood the sublime origin of human existence in the right way can go on living without absorbing this knowledge as a constant source of living joy. If you want to do loving deeds, let the truth about the stupendous origin and destiny of humankind shine out from your eyes; that is the best way to spread anthroposophy. Our deeds will prove its truth, bringing joy to those around us, and having an uplifting, cheering, refreshing and health-giving effect on us in spirit, soul and body. We should be better, healthier and stronger people through taking in anthroposophical thoughts.

The most important thing is that a series of lectures such as this should work in this way. It should be a germinal force which, on entering the soul of the hearer, springs forth and bears fruit for those around us. Although physically we go our separate ways, anthroposophists remain united in spirit. Let us collaborate in that we translate this teaching into life. Let us be filled with this spirit without weakening, until the moment arrives when we come together not only in spirit but meet again in the flesh!

Lecture 11, 16 August 1910[1]

The Portal of Initiation

We are about to begin an important series of lectures, and I am sure it is permissible to tell you beforehand that we could not have undertaken them without all the work already achieved in the anthroposophical field. Another thing is that the momentous ideas to which we shall be devoting ourselves over the coming days need, in a certain respect, the kind of mood we were able to acquire from seeing the two dramas which have just been performed. These performances were meant to give our hearts the kind of feeling mood necessary for us to bring the right warmth and intensity into what comes towards us in the anthroposophical realm. There have been many occasions when I have reminded you that abstract thoughts, even the ideas belonging to our field, acquire their full effect on us only if they are experienced with warm inner feelings. Without these we would not be sensitive enough to realize that with the help of anthroposophical ideas we are approaching areas of existence for which we should not only have intellectual curiosity but also a mood of heart which we can in the fullest sense call a holy mood. It is probably a long time since I had the kind of feelings in my heart, such as I have now, in anticipation of lectures of which we may be justified in saying that they venture to bring human thoughts a little way towards the primordial word which for millennia has taken hold of human hearts and occupied human minds, and which raises human beings in heart and mind to the highest, most sublime heights to which they can aspire, to the majesty of our own origins.

After the past two days, which have prepared us for these lectures, may I be permitted, before they begin, to touch on an intimate aspect of our anthroposophical work. At the start of last year's talks[2] I was already able to point out the symbolic importance these particular Munich performances have for our anthroposophical life. I stressed the way we have been carried for years by what we could call, in a real anthroposophical sense, the patience of waiting until the forces required for the task have matured. Let me remind you once again that *The Children of Lucifer*, which we were fortunate enough to be able to perform last year and, to our joy, repeat this year, had to be patiently awaited for seven years. This play had to be preceded by seven years of work in the field of anthroposophy. I had the opportunity to remind you last year that at the conclusion of the founding of our German Section in Berlin I gave a lecture in conjunction with this play *The Children of Lucifer*, and that in those days the idea of being able to present this play on the stage was still an ideal. After seven years of anthroposophical work this has now happened, and we may say that the performance last year signified a kind of milestone in our anthroposophical activities. We were able to present our dear friends with an artistic development of anthroposophical feeling and thinking. It is in moments such as these, when we feel ourselves surrounded and filled with anthroposophical life, that we feel we have really found our anthroposophical milieu. The author of *The Children of Lucifer*, whom we had the pleasure of seeing here last year at the performance and the lectures and whose presence we are enjoying again this year, has in his epoch-making work *The Great Initiates* presented the spiritual life of today with the kind of web of ideas the effect of which on the hearts and minds of the people of the present day only the future will set in the right light.[3]

You would often be surprised if you were to look at the

estimation people have today of the spiritual powers and spiritual achievements of one past age or another and compare it with the way the people of those times actually saw themselves. We very easily confuse the way we ourselves think of Goethe, Shakespeare or Dante with the kind of insight their contemporaries had for perceiving the spiritual forces individuals such as these men embodied in the developing spirit of humankind. Especially as anthroposophists we must make ourselves aware of the fact that in their own time people can appreciate least of all the significant and strengthening effect the spiritual endeavours of their contemporaries have on human souls. If you bear in mind how differently things will be judged in the future than they are today, you may perhaps say that the time will come when *The Great Initiates* will be regarded, both for its content and its depth, as a work of colossal significance. For already today soul echoes are being heard throughout the widest field of culture precisely because these ideas have found entry into the hearts of our contemporaries. And indeed these echoes are surely important for our contemporaries; to innumerable people they have meant support in life, consolation and hope in the hardest moments of their existence. Only if we can really rejoice over the intellectual and spiritual feats of the present day do we have the right to say that we possess anthroposophical sensitivity and an anthroposophical mood on a somewhat grander scale. The characters who appear in *The Children of Lucifer* have also received their shape and form from out of the same soul depths whence came the ideas in *The Great Initiates*, and these characters present our inner eye with a view of an eminent period in the evolution of humankind when what had grown old and what was newly bursting into life encounter one another. Anthroposophists should understand the way two elements come together: human life, work and action on the physical plane as presented by the characters we see in *The*

Children of Lucifer and, shedding its light into this work and action, what we call illumination from higher worlds. By putting a drama on the stage showing not only that human striving and human capacities are rooted in our hearts and heads, but also that inspiration from the initiation centres of the temple, as invisible powers, inspire and spiritualize our hearts—by showing this interweaving of supersensible worlds with our sense world we have been able to set up a milestone in our anthroposophical movement.

It should be said again this year at the start of our lectures that the essential part of such an undertaking are the hearts of those who have the insight to understand such a work. A great mistake in our times is to think that once a work has been created it is bound to have an effect as such. It does not depend solely on the great works of Raphael or Michelangelo being in the world, it depends on the existence in this world of human beings in whose hearts and souls the magic of these works can be brought to life. Raphael and Michelangelo did not create their works for themselves alone, they did them in response to those of their contemporaries who were filled with the culture of the times, and were capable of receiving what they had committed to the canvas. Our present culture is chaotic; it has no integrity of feeling. However great the masterpieces might be that affect our culture, they will not touch our hearts. It must be a singular characteristic of our anthroposophical movement that we are a circle of friends who share the same feelings, are inspired by the same thoughts, and are capable of the same enthusiasm. A drama takes place on the stage, and in the hearts of the spectators a drama takes place the forces of which belong to time. What the hearts of the audience felt, what took root in every heart, is a seed for the life of the future. Let us feel this, my dear friends, but let us make sure we do not only feel a sense of satisfaction, for that might be a bit shabby. But let us be aware of the responsibility we are taking on board, the kind of responsibility that tells us to set an example for what has to happen, what has to become possible so that the culture of the times becomes impregnated with an awareness of the human being here on the physical plane being a mediator between physical deeds and physical development on the one hand and the forces from the supersensible world which can enter into these realms of the physical plane only through human beings.

In a sense we shall only become a spiritual family if we turn towards the general primordial principle of the Father which lives in our hearts and which I have just been trying to characterize. If we do take up with our hearts, with our whole mood of soul, what we experience, feeling ourselves as members of our anthroposophical family, then we shall really appreciate with the warmest inner satisfaction our good fortune in being able to have the author of *The Children of Lucifer* with us for the two performances and the days to follow.

What I am saying is that this will really enable us to feel that the living anthroposophical forces of the present day are alive in the circle from which such works as we have experienced in the last couple of days have come.

My dear friends, last year I already took up the pleasant duty of drawing your attention to the very place of work in which we have been able to achieve such a milestone of our anthroposophical activities, and I would like to emphasize that you must not understand duty in its ordinary everyday meaning. It was a duty which was a labour of love—and I stress the word 'love'—it was and is a labour of love to be able to say again at this moment in time that for the successful realization of these our anthroposophical events our friends worked not only eagerly but with all their strength and all their devotion.

When you see performances like these you may not always realize how long it takes until what can finally be presented in a few hours becomes fit to perform. And the manner in which our dear friends co-operated to bring the production about could well be taken as a model of anthroposophical work, possibly even of human co-operation altogether. Particularly when we consider that it would go against a proper anthroposophical feeling to give orders in any way in this sort of work. It is only possible to go ahead if the individuals are wholeheartedly involved in quite a different way than could happen in a similar artistic field outside. Moreover, this wholehearted involvement existed not only in the few short weeks at our disposal for preparing the performances, for this loving, voluntary co-operation has gone on for years. On this occasion people have come together from far and wide—and anthroposophists do not only want to get to know one another through exchanging just a few words but want to find out about everyone else's deepest ideals. Thus it is right to draw your attention in a few words to the way people have been working here for years so as to bring together at the right moment what was required to set going the kind of achievement which we have just been able to present. Even if it were not called for by outer circumstances alone, my heart would urge me to take this opportunity to draw your attention to the devoted work of our friends who have made it possible for us to have these experiences. For believe me, without this devoted work it would not have been possible.

As I said, I want to begin these lectures with a kind of intimate discussion of something that can be close to our hearts. Let us remember first and foremost the years of dedicated work of the two ladies who have been working so purposefully and with such sensitivity for our anthroposophical intentions. For many years now Fräulein Stinde and Countess Kalckreuth have devoted all their forces to the anthroposophical work going on here.[4] And I am the best judge of the fact that the event we were able to lay on to our satisfaction would not have been possible without their dedicated, purposeful help that has been in such harmony with our anthroposophical impulses. Therefore you will find it all the more comprehensible that I am availing myself of this opportunity to say these few words to our two colleagues here in Munich with a very grateful heart. In addition to this there were the people who were keeping everything going with such devotion during the weeks while our activities were taking place.

Yesterday we endeavoured by way of an artistic picture to set before you the path to the heights on which the human being can experience what should be inherent in anthroposophical development, and what so to speak a spiritual investigator ought to experience.[5] The opportunity may present itself in connection with various things that will be said during these lectures to refer to one thing or another that was presented to you yesterday. We endeavoured to show the life of someone aspiring towards spiritual knowledge; to show how he grows out of the physical plane, how even here on the physical plane everything that happens around him, and which might seem really mundane to another person, is of importance to him. The soul of the spiritual seeker has to grow out of the soil of the events of the physical plane. We then endeavoured to show what the soul has to experience within itself when everything going on around us in the way of human destiny, human suffering and joy, human striving and illusion pours into it; how the soul can be crushed and shattered, and yet the power of wisdom can work its way through this destruction until in the moment when the human being believes that he has at last become a stranger to the sense world, he is approached by the really big illusions.

With the words 'the world is *maya* or illusion', or 'through knowledge we find our way to wisdom' we say a lot, and yet very little. What these words are actually saying has to be experienced by each individual in his own way. Therefore, what applies in general could only be shown with a genuine soul force pulsating through it if it were to be shown in the form of an individual's own experience. What has to be shown is not how everyone approaches the region of initiation but the way the absolutely individual character of Johannes Thomasius, out of his own particular circumstances, is able to approach the gates of knowledge. It would be totally wrong if someone were to believe that he could consider the occurrence shown in the meditation room, of Maria ascending out of her body into devachan, as a general one. It is an absolutely real, spiritually real happening, but one that should show the impulse to ascend to the spiritual world in the particular way a personality such as that of Johannes Thomasius demonstrates.

I want to draw your special attention to the moment when we are shown that at the very instant when his soul has basically acquired the force to see through ordinary illusion it is exposed to the possibility of the really big illusions. Imagine Johannes Thomasius not being in a position to realize—not even just sensing it with his inner eye, let alone in any way consciously—that in the character left behind in the meditation room and hurling a curse at the hierophant the very individuality he is meant to follow is no longer present. Imagine the hierophant, or even Johannes Thomasius, becoming agitated by this even for a moment. It would then have become impossible for an incalculable span of time that Johannes Thomasius could continue on the path of knowledge. The whole thing would have been over at that moment, and not only for Johannes Thomasius but also for the hierophant, who would then not have been capable of developing in Johannes Thomasius the strong forces which can lead him beyond this obstacle. The hierophant would have had to resign from his office, and tremendously long spans of time would have been lost to Johannes Thomasius in his progress.

If you try to visualize the scenes that immediately precede this moment and the feelings going on in the soul of Johannes Thomasius, the particular type of pain, the particular kind of experience, then you may perhaps come to the conclusion that even if he may not be aware of it himself, the power of wisdom has become so strong in him that he can surmount this tremendous jolt. All these experiences taking place without anything visibly hovering before the inner eye of the soul, have to happen first, so that they can be adequately followed up by what comes next: namely the spiritual world showing the soul something which, even if it is initially in picture form, is nevertheless objective. This happens in the following scenes. First of all his whole person is thoroughly shaken by pain, by the violent emotion coming from his having withstood the possibility of a great illusion. All this works itself into a tremendous tension in the soul which, if we can describe it this way, reverses the gaze, so that what was only subjective before can now appear to the soul with the force of objectivity.

What you see in the following scenes, and which I have attempted to describe in a spiritually realistic way, presents what the person developing gradually into higher worlds feels to be the outer mirror image of the feelings he experienced first of all in his soul, and what is true, without his yet knowing fully how much of it is true. The human being is first of all led upwards so that he can see how time in which we dwell as sensory beings is, with regard to its causes and effects, bordered on all sides by other domains. You see not only the small section of it presented by the sense world but you come to understand that what appears before us in the sense world is only the outer expression of spirit. Therefore, with his spiritual eye Johannes Thomasius sees the man whom he has first met on the physical plane, Capesius, not as he is now, but as he was decades ago as a young man. And he sees the other one, Strader, not in the form he has at present, but he has a premonition of what he will be like if he continues to develop in the way he is doing up to the present. We understand this moment only when we can stretch it beyond the present, both into the past and into the future. Then we approach the realm with which everything happening in the present is connected as with spiritual threads; then the spiritual world comes to meet us, the spiritual world with which the human being always has a relationship even if he is not capable of grasping it with his ordinary physical intellect and ordinary sensuousness.

Believe me, it is no mere image or symbol but a realistic description in the scene in which the young Capesius describes his ideals with the kind of heartiness which would be justified in the sense world—ideals which, where the spiritual world is concerned, have the peculiarity that after all they have their roots in the external world perceived by the senses. It is absolutely realistic when we are shown that what he and Strader say stirs up the elements and unleashes lightning and thunder. The human being is not an isolated being. What a human being expresses in words, activates in thoughts, experiences in feelings, is connected to the whole cosmos, and every word, every feeling and every thought, continues. Without a human being knowing it his mistakes, his untrue feelings, work destructively in the elemental realm of our existence. And what anyone going along this path of knowledge needs to be sure to learn from these preliminary experiences in the spiritual world is a profound sense of responsibility which says: 'What you do as a human being is not confined to the isolated spot where your lips move, where you think and where your heart beats: it is part of all the world. If it is productive, then it is productive for the whole world; if it is a destructive error, it is a destructive force in the whole world.'

Everything we experience in this way on our ascent works further in our soul. If it works in the right way it bears us upwards into higher regions of spiritual life, as I have endeavoured to describe in the devachanic realm into which the soul of Maria along with her companions has gone on ahead of Johannes Thomasius. Take it as a spiritual reality and not as an abstract thought when I tell you that these three helpers, Philia, Astrid and Luna, are the forces which, *in abstracto*, when we are speaking from the point of view of the physical plane, we call the sentient soul, the intellectual soul and the consciousness soul. But do not succumb to the illusion that anything is achieved if you try in an artistically conceived production to symbolize the characters by means of abstract concepts. That is not what is intended. They are meant to be real characters, active forces. You will not find notice boards in devachan with sentient soul, intellectual soul and consciousness soul written on them but real beings, as real for the spirit world as any human being of flesh and blood can be for the physical plane. A human being ought to be aware of the fact that he robs things of their content if he tries to define everything in abstract symbolism. In the world in which Johannes Thomasius has hitherto been active he has only experienced what you could call the spiritual world spread out before his soul in picture form. Whether he himself as a subjective being is the author of this world or whether it is founded in truth he has not been capable of deciding up to now. How much of this world is illusion and how much is reality he has to decide for the first time now that he has come into that exalted region in which he meets with the soul of Maria.

Try imagining that one night after you have gone to sleep you are suddenly transported into quite a different world, and you cannot find in this other world one single point of reference that links up with your previous experiences. Then you would not be the same person, the same being. You must have the chance of taking something over into the other world and seeing it again there, in order to guarantee truth. You can only do this in the case of the spiritual world if you have already acquired a firm foothold that assures you of the truth. In this dramatic presentation this is intended to be provided for in that on the physical plane Johannes Thomasius is connected with Maria's being not only through his emotions and passions but in the depths of his heart, so that a spiritual connection already exists on the physical plane. This is the only way in which this friendship could be the kind of focal point in the spiritual world that confirms the truth of everything else within it. The certainty of truth radiates out over everything else in the spiritual world because Johannes Thomasius finds a foothold which he has discovered in the physical world in a different way than through the mere illusions of sensuousness or intellect. This links the two worlds together for him, and makes him sufficiently mature to be able to spread his memory in reality over past lives, and in doing so to grow in soul beyond the sense world as we know it.

This is why, at this point, something occurs which, if we may put it this way, embraces a certain mystery of the spiritual world. Theodora who, on the physical plane, sees into the future and is able to foresee the momentous event beginning to occur, the re-appearance of the Christ, is capable, on the spiritual plane, of calling up a vision of the significance of past events. If we are going to give a realistic portrayal we have to present it in the spiritual world as it really happens. For the beings dwelling in devachan, the past, with the significance its forces have for them, is enhanced because in that region the forces that are becoming active there are the opposite of the forces we perceive here on the physical plane as the forces of prophecy. It is a realistic description when Theodora who, on the physical plane, can prophesy the future is, on the spiritual plane, the conscience and memory-awakener for what has happened in the past, and thus brings about the moment through which Johannes Thomasius looks back into his own past to when he was already connected with the individuality of Maria. This prepares him, in his further life, to go through everything that will lead him to a conscious recognition of the spiritual world. And you will see how, on the one hand, the soul changes into something quite different when subjected to the experiences of spiritual worlds, how everything appears in a new light. You will see how what used to bring us pain and distress is, when we experience it as another self in our own self, a source of comfort and hope, how the experience of being poured out into the world makes us large and significant; and we see how the human being grows into those parts of the cosmos. But we also see that human beings may on no account become arrogant, for error—the possibility of error—has by no means disappeared yet, and Johannes Thomasius, despite the fact that he has already acquired a great deal of insight into spiritual worlds, can have at that moment the spiritual sensation that the devil incarnate is coming through the door, whereas actually his greatest benefactor, Benedictus, is approaching.

Just as this is possible on the spiritual plane, so are innumerable other illusions of the greatest variety. Do not let anyone be intimidated by this; on the contrary, let it be a warning that where the spiritual world is concerned everyone must on the one hand apply discretion and on the other hand face the possibility of error bravely and boldly and on no account allow himself to become despondent if anything appears in any way that shows itself to be an erroneous report from a spiritual world. The human being has to go through all these things in a real way if he really wants to reach what one can call the temple of knowledge, if he wants to ascend to a real understanding of the four great powers of the world which in a certain respect guide and lead world destiny and which are represented by the four hierophants of the temple.

If we preserve the feeling that the soul has to go through things like this before it is capable of perceiving how the sense world comes forth from the spiritual world, and if we attune ourselves not to want to describe the foundations of the world with ordinary commonplace words but want in the first place to acquire an insight into the inner value of the words, then we shall sense the significance of the primordial words which are used at the beginning of the Bible to describe the creation. We must feel the necessity to let go of the usual meaning we carry in us of the words 'heaven and earth', 'create', 'light and darkness' and all the other words. We have to let go of the feeling we have in our ordinary life with regard to these words and have to take steps in the direction of resolving to rise to new levels of feeling, a new evaluation of words when we attend these lectures, so that we hear not only what the ideas convey but hear the words telling us what they really mean, and where we will only reach what comes to us out of dark regions of the world with a soul mood properly attuned.

I have endeavoured to sketch for you, in very few words, what we showed you yesterday. It was shown under relatively difficult circumstances, and in addition was only possible because of the loyal and devoted work of a number of our anthroposophical friends. Now allow me to express what I wish to say from the depths of my heart, namely that I myself, and no doubt everyone who knows about it, cannot thank all those people enough who have worked with us and shared the risk of putting on this attempt—for an attempt was all it was meant to be. The circumstances under which we dared make the attempt were certainly not the easiest. Those who took part had worked hard for weeks, and this last week called for their total commitment and dedication. And we can consider it a great achievement of our anthroposophical activities that we have artists among us who have already been giving us their loyal artistic support for two whole years. Let us be sure to remember our dear friend Doser, who not only last year and this year took on the difficult task of representing Phosphoros on the stage, but who has also taken upon himself this year a part which is particularly dear to my heart, and which was infinitely important in what we were attempting to show yesterday: the part of Capesius. Perhaps it will only gradually dawn on you why the figure of Capesius is of such particular importance. And the other figure, too, the character of Strader, acted by our dear Seiling, who has supported us faithfully for two years now, is also of great importance, especially in this context. I must not omit to mention what a great support our dear Herr Seiling is with his unique voice, when it comes to conveying symbolically the spiritual world in the physical world. All the love and the wonderfully pleasing sound of the spirit voices we owe to his quite extraordinary gift in this direction.[6]

It also falls to me to give special thanks to those who put their whole strength into acting the main parts, despite the fact that they had a number of other things to do in the anthroposophical field during this time and actually the whole year through. We can perhaps say that it is only in the anthroposophical field that anyone can muster the amount of strength that Fräulein von Sivers did to play two such big parts, Cleonice and Maria, in two successive days. Such a thing is only possible if you put the utmost strength into it that a person can muster. I would like to mention with a particularly grateful heart the lady who took the part of Johannes Thomasius, and it would give me special satisfaction if we were to think of this role of Johannes Thomasius as still being somewhat connected with the first person who acted the part. That it was possible to do it at all under the difficult circumstances is due solely to the intense dedication our dear

Fräulein Waller has for the anthroposophical cause. And if I were to tell you about the difficulties she had to work under due to shortage of time, you would probably be very surprised. All these things taking place among us, arising out of our anthroposophical work, affect us all because in a spiritual sense we are an anthroposophical family. So we should feel duty bound to thank all those who devoted themselves with such dedication to this task which—always bearing in mind that outsiders are incapable of judging the difficult circumstances—nobody else could possibly have done. May these words enable you to appreciate the heights of dedication to which, over the past days and weeks, the actors have risen, and therefore how justified we are in expressing our deepest thanks just now.

I would have to go on for a very long time if I were to thank individually everyone who joined with us in this work. But let us be sure to remember the man who, when it comes to someone in our ranks doing something for the anthroposophical cause, is always on the spot with the appropriate solution, and gives it with all his heart and all his ability; let us think of our dear friend Arenson who, both last year and this time, supported us with his beautiful musical skills and made it possible that both in *The Children of Lucifer* and in our endeavours of yesterday we could, in the appropriate places, lead over in a most dignified manner to an experience that can only be reached through the world of sound.[7] And let me remind you of our dear artistic friends in Munich. You have had plenty of opportunity over these two days to see how we strove to bring everything seen by the eye into harmony with the spoken word and the music. You will have seen how down to the last splash of colour and every last form we strove to integrate it all. If we achieved this to any extent we owe it to the loving understanding of our artistic friends here, Herr Volkert, Herr Linde and our dear Herr Hass, and we give them our heartiest thanks for doing all they did to enable everything to run its course in such an admirable way.

Such things are only possible of course when everyone's work is given freely with heartfelt devotion. This year, too, we should give a special thought to all that was needed in the way of costumes. It is difficult to imagine all that this entails; but to do this properly it was a job demanding a person's whole time, a person's whole heart and soul. And, as last year, too, the person to take on this load all by herself was our dear Fräulein von Eckhardtstein. She threw herself into the work not only with devotion but, most importantly, with the greatest understanding for both the individual details and the overall dignified impression which must never be neglected.

However, these are only rough indications of what had to be said out of the feeling of being an anthroposophical family, so that each one of us realizes the driving power behind this team work. If the day before yesterday and yesterday you acquired a little satisfaction for your soul, and stimulus for your imagination, then let these feelings overflow a little bit in the direction of the people whose names have just been mentioned, and to your familiar friends who appeared on the stage.

We would like to think of this milestone of our anthroposophical activity as a flow of anthroposophical ideas, anthroposophical life, into culture. Even if modern humanity is not yet inclined to include in all the rest of external culture what can flow into it from out of the life of the spirit, we would like at least to show in an artistic picture the way the thoughts active in our souls can come alive. Feelings such as these can be sparked off through the anticipation of the fact that human beings will move from the present towards a future when they will be able to feel the streaming down of spiritual life through spiritual and soul veins on to the physical plane, that humankind will go towards a future in which human beings will feel themselves to be mediators between the spiritual and the physical world. These events were undertaken just so that this presentiment could awaken.

If we have this kind of presentiment then we will also find it possible to restore the original glory to words which have become so worn out that the feelings they engender now block the way to an understanding of their real significance. No one at all will be able to understand the stupendous content of the words with which the Bible opens if he takes them in the way they are used nowadays. We ourselves will have to soar up in thought to those heights where spiritual life pulsates and to which we tried to follow Johannes Thomasius, if we want to understand physical life on earth. In a certain respect quite a different language has to be spoken in these spiritual realms. However, we human beings must at the least be able to give to the words available to us here quite new values, new nuances of feeling, and have quite a different awareness of them, if they are to signify what the opening passages of the Bible are saying, and if we want to understand the spiritual origin of our physical world.

Notes

Lecture 1

1   The first lecture in this series, given on 16 August 1910, was devoted chiefly to thanking all those who had made possible the preceding presentation of dramas by Edouard Schuré and Rudolf Steiner. Since it does not address the theme of the series it has been included at the end of the book.

2   Speaking here in 1910, Rudolf Steiner was still using the term 'theosophy' to denote what he later came to call 'anthroposophy' or 'spiritual science'. He himself wished these latter terms to be used in later editions of his earlier lectures.

3   בְּרֵאשִׁית בָּרָא אֱלֹהִים אֵת הַשָּׁמַיִם וְאֵת הָאָרֶץ׃

4   R. Steiner *An Outline of Esoteric Science* (GA 13), Anthroposophic Press, New York 1997.

5   *bet*: בּ,   *resh*: ר,   *shin*: שׁ.

Lecture 2

1   תֹהוּ וָבֹהוּ

2   רוּחַ אֱלֹהִים מְרַחֶפֶת

3   רָחַף

Lecture 3

1   רָקִיעַ

2   R. Steiner 'The Portal of Initiation. A Rosicrucian Mystery' in *Four Mystery Dramas* (GA 14), Rudolf Steiner Press, London 1997.

Lecture 4

1 R. Steiner *An Occult Physiology* (GA 128), Rudolf Steiner Press 1983.

2 יוֹם

3 R. Steiner *The Mission of the Individual Folk Souls in Relation to Teutonic Mythology* (GA 121), Rudolf Steiner Press, London 1970.

4 *erev*: עֶרֶב   *boker*: בֹּקֶר

Lecture 5

1 רוּחַ אֱלֹהִים

2 J. Fletcher (Ed.) *Goethe's Approach to Colour*, Rudolf Steiner Press, London 1977.

3 R. Steiner 'The Portal of Initiation, A Rosicrucian Mystery' in *Four Mystery Dramas*, op. cit.

4 לַיְלָה

5 R. Steiner *The Mission of the Individual Folk Souls*, op. cit.

Lecture 6

1 R. Steiner 'The Portal of Initiation. A Rosicrucian Mystery' in *Four Mystery Dramas*, op. cit.

2 יְהוָה אֱלֹהִים

Lecture 7

1 This journal was published by Rudolf Steiner from 1903 to 1908. The essays referred to here are in *Cosmic Memory. Atlantis and Lemuria* (GA 11), Garber Communications, New York 1990.

2 R. Steiner 'The Portal of Initiation. A Rosicrucian Mystery' in *Four Mystery Dramas*, op. cit.

3 J. Fletcher (Ed.) *Goethe's Approach to Colour*, op. cit.

Lecture 9

1   R. Steiner *The Mission of the Individual Folk Souls*, op. cit.

Lecture 10

1   Genesis I, 21 & 24: נֶפֶשׁ חַיָּה

2   Genesis II, 7.

3   נְשָׁמָה

4   φθείρεσθαι

5   תּוֹלְדוֹת

6   Genesis X, 1.

7   Maximilian Gümbel-Seiling (1879–1964), actor and speech artist who played the role of Strader in Rudolf Steiner's mystery plays.

8   Ludwig Deinhard *Das Mysterium des Menschen im Lichte der psychischen Forschung. Eine Einführung in den Okkultismus*, Berlin 1910.

9   Jakob Boehme (1575–1624), mystic and philosopher. See R. Steiner *Mystics after Modernism* (GA 7), Anthroposophic Press, New York 2000.

Lecture 11

1   See Lecture 1, Note 1.

2   R. Steiner *The East in the Light of the West* (GA 113), Garber Communications, New York 1986.

3   Edouard Schuré (1841–1912), French historian and dramatist.

4   With her friend Pauline von Kalckreuth (1856–1929), Sophie Stinde (1853–1915) led the Munich group of the Theosophical Society from 1907 to 1913 and was the main organizer of the Society's mystery drama performances there. See the lectures Rudolf Steiner gave in Stuttgart after her death on 22, 23 and 24

November 1915 in R. Steiner *Die Geistigen Hintergründe des Ersten Weltkrieges*, Vol. VIII (GA 174b), Dornach 1994.

5 'The Portal of Initiation. A Rosicrucian Mystery' in *Four Mystery Dramas*, op. cit.

6 See Note 7 to Lecture 10.

7 Adolf Arenson (1855–1936). The music he composed for Rudolf Steiner's four mystery dramas was published by Verlag Freies Geistesleben in 1961 in an arrangement for piano by Léon Mouravieff.

Note Regarding Rudolf Steiner's Lectures

The lectures and addresses contained in this volume have been translated from the German, which is based on stenographic and other recorded texts that were in most cases never seen or revised by the lecturer. Hence, due to human errors in hearing and transcription, they may contain mistakes and faulty passages. Every effort has been made to ensure that this is not the case. Some of the lectures were given to audiences more familiar with anthroposophy; these are the so-called 'private' or 'members' lectures. Other lectures, like the written works, were intended for the general public. The difference between these, as Rudolf Steiner indicates in his *Autobiography*, is twofold. On the one hand, the members' lectures take for granted a background in and commitment to anthroposophy; in the public lectures this was not the case. At the same time, the members' lectures address the concerns and dilemmas of the members, while the public work speaks directly out of Steiner's own understanding of universal needs. Nevertheless, as Rudolf Steiner stresses: 'Nothing was ever said that was not solely the result of my direct experience of the growing content of anthroposophy. There was never any question of concessions to the prejudices and preferences of the members. Whoever reads these privately printed lectures can take them to represent anthroposophy in the fullest sense. Thus it was possible without hesitation—when the complaints in this direction became too persistent—to depart from the custom of circulating this material "For members only". But it must be borne in mind that faulty passages do occur in these reports not revised by myself.' Earlier in the same chapter, he states: 'Had I been able to correct them [the private lectures], the restriction *for members only* would have been unnecessary from the beginning.'

The original German editions on which this text is based were published by Rudolf Steiner Verlag, Dornach, Switzerland in the collected edition (*Gesamtausgabe*, 'GA') of Rudolf Steiner's work. All publications are edited by the Rudolf Steiner Nachlassverwaltung (estate), which wholly owns both Rudolf Steiner Verlag and the Rudolf Steiner Archive. The organization relies solely on donations to continue its activity.

For further information please contact:

Rudolf Steiner Archiv
Postfach 135
CH-4143 Dornach

or:

www.rudolf-steiner.com